While every precaution has been ⟨

publisher assumes no responsibility for errors or omissions, or for damage resulting from the use of the information contained herein.

THE FINANCIAL GUIDELINE TO PROSPERITY, FINANCIAL SE-CURITY, AND WELLNESS

First edition. June 26, 2023.

Table of Contents

THE FINANCIAL GUIDELINE TO PROSPERITY, FINANCIAL SECURITY, AND WELLNESS

CONTACT US

FRANK BONHOMME

TEL: 901-657-5913

FAX: 888-758-9639

Www.thefinancialguidelines.com[1]

Info@thefinancialguidelines.com

Address: 237-33 Jamaica Avenue

Bellerose, NY 11426

ILLUSTRATION

BY

KALIYAH BONHOMME

FOREWORD

By Chantell Davidson

When considering the concept of Generational Wealth, commonly associated with families like Rockefeller's, Kennedy's, Vanderbilt's, and Hilton's, it becomes evident that none of these prominent examples are black families. Throughout American history, black families have struggled and fought for freedom, civil rights, and recognition of their humanity. Unfortunately, due to the ongoing battle for equality, the essential teachings of financial independence have been overlooked and neglected within today's generation of black communities. Although figures like Madame CJ Walker have achieved wealth in their time, their families have not been able to sustain that legacy. The idea of generational wealth thus feels distant for our demographic, as negative perceptions inherited from previous generations have hindered progress. Current generations are only discovering financial literacy and growth later in life through trial and error but imagine the potential if this knowledge were instilled at a younger age. This book has the power to effectuate such a change by providing comprehensive knowledge and tools that go beyond the surface-level financial literacy taught in schools. It aims to guide younger generations towards pursuing financial growth through various avenues, ensuring that both growth and knowledge are passed down more effectively. With emphasis on the significance of leaving a legacy, Frank Bonhomme's work goes beyond the mere transmission of a family name. This is particularly crucial for black communities, where the encouragement and development of financial literacy, independence, growth, and knowledge have not been prioritized as they should be. The empowerment offered by this book will be invaluable to current and future generations, establishing a golden legacy that will endure for years to come.

FOREWORD

By Rich Vasquez

Frank Bonhomme, whose name translates to "Good Man," exemplifies his name through his actions as a family man, community leader, and man of faith. His primary objective has always been to uplift the community by breaking cultural barriers, particularly for the new generation of professionals and entrepreneurs who support themselves, their families, and their clients.

While Frank initially specialized in providing exceptional accounting and tax expertise, his practice has expanded to offer a range of services that impact the lives of his clients at various stages of their financial journey. Whether he is guiding them through the process of buying their first home or assisting them as they transition into parenthood, Frank advises many clients during their "builder phase," ensuring they receive the proper guidance needed to achieve their goals and objectives.

As his client's progress beyond the builder phase into the "wealth accumulation phase," Frank continues to provide valuable advice. These individuals, often professionals and business owners, require sound guidance to scale and grow their endeavors without worrying about business, financial, or penalty risks. Frank serves as a reliable sounding board for these individuals, helping them strategize and overcome challenges on their path to greater success.

Frank's support does not end there. During the "wealth distribution" phase, he remains by his clients' side, ensuring a smooth transition into the next stage of their lives. By helping them plan for various "what-if" scenarios, Frank ensures that unforeseen interruptions do not result in devastating losses but instead facilitate positive rebounding.

Frank serves as a shining example to all, demonstrating that prioritizing service often leads to success for all involved in the journey. As a partner, mentor, and community leader, Frank has earned the gratitude of numerous families and business owners. Let us raise a toast to his continued efforts, ensuring that the next generation carries forward his remarkable legacy.

THIS BOOK IS DEDICATED TO MY MOTHER MARIE SOLIDE SAINVIL

The woman who brought me into this world not only gave me life but also sacrificed so much for us. Mom, your tireless efforts to provide for us and accomplish so much as a single parent are truly appreciated. Thank you for always loving me, praying for me, and guiding me. Although you are no longer with me, I still hold the valuable lessons you taught me close to my heart and try to live by them. Your presence is still felt, and you continue to inspire me to do better in life and treat others with kindness. I wish you were here to witness the fruits of your labor that you cultivated, but your memory will forever live on in my heart. You are dearly missed.

AUTHOR BIO

Frank Bonhomme is a self-made businessman and financial social media host with a lifelong passion for finance. He recently made his debut as an author, marking his first foray into the world of writing. Frank holds a bachelor's degree in accountancy from Long Island University and an associate degree in business administration from Nassau Community College. Currently, he is pursuing a JD law degree at Novus Law School. Alongside his academic pursuits, Frank also works as a financial advisor, real estate agent, accountant, and insurance broker. He is a devoted husband and proud father of two children.

Table of Contents

INTRODUCTION

Welcome to *The Financial Guideline to Prosperity, Financial Security, and Wellness,* a book that has been meticulously crafted with the sole aim of helping you, the reader, succeed in your financial endeavors. Before we delve into any of our research-backed financial advice, allow me to share my qualifications in the realm of finance. Since embarking on my journey as a real estate agent at the age of 25, I have accumulated over two decades of experience in the industry, alongside which I have gained valuable insights into the mortgage sector through work as a junior loan officer. Having subsequently ventured to the depths of insurance, finance, and tax industry—establishing my own successful accounting practice in the latter—I have been empowered with a rare appreciation for the interconnectedness that unites all facets of the financial world. It is this secret that I hope to share with you through this book, in which I will connect various financial topics and elaborate on key principles that are crucial for financial literacy.

Finance plays an incredibly significant role in our lives, yet it remains regrettably overlooked by the curriculums of inner-city grade schools. Since financial literacy is often introduced at the college level, one may reasonably ponder whether this lack of early education is by design. We may question, perhaps, who truly benefits from a financially uninformed populace. It is not fair to say that grade school curriculums cease to evolve; outdated programs like woodworking and mechanics have been cut in recent decades. Rather, financial education appears to be selectively left behind. I firmly believe that providing financial knowledge to individuals, particularly high school graduates, equips them with essential skills such as budgeting, saving, bill payment, and credit management. Since an opportunity or desire to attend college is not universal among our population, teaching our youth about finance at a young age is pivotal to the cultivation of habits and skills that will benefit them throughout their lives. While it of course remains advisable to seek the guidance of a qualified accountant or financial advisor in more specialist scansions, I strongly believe that individuals seeking financial assistance should possess, as a minimum, the basic knowledge needed to prevent exploitation.

Now, you might wonder why I have chosen to write a book about prosperity, financial security, and wellness. To answer this inquiry, let is begin by examining the definitions of these three terms. *Prosperity* refers to the state of achieving success and possessing substantial wealth. *Financial security* implies that one holds sufficient resources to cover expenses, emergencies, and retirement without the constant fear of running out of funds. *Wellness*, on the other hand, refers to being in good health and actively pursuing this health as a short- and long-term goal. One may ponder whether it is possible to attain all three simultaneously. Certainly, instinct tells us that countless hours spent working tirelessly to achieve prosperity may ultimately prove detrimental to one's health. The saying "the more money, the more problems" comes to mind, harnessing implications that those who have succeeded in gaining prosperity subsequently find themselves perpetually on guard against those who may threaten it. We often hear stories of celebrities or lottery winners who come into sudden wealth, only to squander it within a few years or months. They were once prosperous but now find themselves nearly destitute, falling from prosperity to financial insecurity in a metaphorical blink of the eye. One can exceed their means in terms of prosperity but, in the absence of informed financial guidance, it can all be lost. Our aim, then, should be to prosper in wealth, health, and peace. It is this aim that is reflected in the title of this book.

Throughout our financial journey through these pages, we will explore various aspects of finance, recognizing its interconnectedness with every facet of our lives. From the moment we are born, our parents begin planning for our future, but those plans require financial resources. Whether it's saving for our first car, college education, wedding, or first home, money permeates every component of our future. Knowing how to manage money is therefore crucial, and I believe it ranks among the most important skills that one can possess, completing something of a 'holy quadrinity' alongside health, education, and family. Again, these aspects are intertwined, and a lack of financial education can introduce significant stress within families or impact our health when we are unable to access suitable housing, food, or healthcare. Furthermore, educational opportunities may suffer due to financial constraints.

Even after reading this book, you will still require the expertise of a financial advisor. After all, we cannot replace years of qualifications over the course of a few hundred pages. What we can do, however, is arm ourselves with the knowledge needed to effectively choose a proficient finance professional specializing in the specific area in which we require assistance. The information contained herein is general in nature, so it is essential to consult a professional who can advise you on your specific circumstances. These tools will also help you hold your financial advisor, tax consultant, mortgage broker, or real estate agent accountable and avoid one of the other great dangers to our financial health: exploitation.

Each book read, job undertaken, and course completed holds significance in one's life, even if the full extent of their impact remains undiscovered. The relentless pursuit of knowledge stands as a fundamental priority throughout our time on Earth. I have personally read countless books and listened to numerous audiobooks, and each of these have contributed to the person I am today. When we examine successful individuals, we find a common thread among them, besides wealth and recognition—they are avid readers. It is essential to note that the financial prosperity discussed in this book does not offer a shortcut to instant wealth. It encompasses the ability to live comfortably in the present, both while working and after retirement. It entails having a financial cushion to weather unexpected events in life. It encompasses leaving a legacy for your family, church, and community.

CHAPTER ONE
THE DIFFERENT MINDSET

Managing one's finances is not solely a manner of adopting the right mindset and habits; it is also about avoiding certain behaviors and actions that can result in that least enviable of outcomes: financial ruin. In this opening section, we will explore some of the common mistakes that people make when it comes to managing their finances, and—most crucially—ascertain methods of how to avoid them.

One of the most common mistakes people make is overspending. This may sound obvious, but we ought to investigate this issue more deeply. Put simply, overspending occurs when individuals spend more money than they earn. Over time, this discrepancy can lead to debt and financial instability. For any number of 'over spenders' you encounter, you may discover an equal number of reasons underlying the reckless financial behavior of these individuals. Be it a lack of budgeting, impulsive spending, or a pressure to maintain pace with the lucrative lifestyles of our peers, causes of overspending vary from person to person. On paper, however, combatting this issue is rather straightforward; We must learn to create a budget, track our expenses, and prioritize our spending to ensure that any expenses are within our means.

Another common mistake is failing to save. Again, this issue can arise from a plethora of reasons, most commonly a lack of discipline or a limited understanding regarding the importance of saving. The latter is particularly concerning, given that saving is essential for building an emergency fund, investing in retirement, or achieving financial goals. To avoid this mistake, then, individuals should prioritize saving-oriented behaviors and adopt a habit of setting aside a certain percentage of their income for savings each month. In other words, we must learn to pay ourselves before paying others.

Investing without proper knowledge and research is another common mistake. Of course, investing can be an effective way to build wealth. In the absence of adequate research and knowledge, however, it can also be decidedly risky. As such, is important that any budding investor takes the time to learn about different investment options, such as stocks, bonds, and mutual funds, and understand the risks associated with each investment option before making a decision. It is also essential to diversify investments to minimize risks.

Failing to pay off debt is another mistake that can create financial problems. Debt can accumulate quickly, and high-interest rates can make it challenging to pay off. Most worryingly, the longer debt remains unpaid, the steeper the hill becomes. Thus, individuals should prioritize paying off high-interest debt first and adopt a strategy for paying off the remaining debt. Consolidating debt and negotiating interest rates with creditors can also help reduce the debt burden.

Finally, failing to plan can lead to financial instability. Finance is not something that we will escape as our lives progress. On the contrary, it is something that becomes increasingly important as we age. Hence, it is essential to plan for retirement, unexpected expenses, and other life events that may impact our financial security. Individuals should develop a long-term financial plan that includes saving, investing, and budgeting for future expenses.

THE BROKE MINDSET

The Broke mindset is embodied by individuals who habitually allocate their entire paycheck towards acquiring assets that depreciate over time. To put it simply, individuals with a Broke mindset invest their hard-earned money in items that do not increase in value as time goes on. Examples of such assets include clothes, shoes, automobiles, and various forms of technology. While these possessions may provide temporary satisfaction and serve immediate needs, they do not—except in exceedingly rare cases—possess the ability to generate long-term financial growth. On the other hand, appreciating assets are those that have the potential to increase in value over time, such as real property, gold and silver, stocks, bonds, and various forms of currency.

To provide a tangible example, I recall a friend from my high school days who was involved in an illicit trade. Despite his substantial income, he fell victim to the Broke mindset. Each week, he would lavishly spend the money he made through this 'work' on an abundance of expensive sneakers, and once revealed that he allocated over $300 toward renewing his stash of undergarments. Astonishingly, he never wore his socks or undergarments more than once, instead opting to discard them after a single use. This excessive and unsustainable behavior perfectly encapsulates the misguided approach of the Broke mindset, where money is spent on depreciating assets without considering their long-term financial implications. Of course, this situation did not end well for the individual in question.

By exploring the pitfalls and consequences associated with the Broke mindset, this book aims to provide invaluable insights into the importance of making wise financial decisions. Through understanding the distinction between assets that appreciate and those that depreciate, readers will be empowered to cultivate a more prosperous and financially sustainable future.

THE PENNY SAVER MINDSET

In the world of personal finance, most of us have encountered at least one individual who possesses an unwavering dedication to saving every penny they earn. It is a trait that we tend to notice in others, and one that collects mixed reception in society. While saving is undoubtedly an important aspect of financial management, it is crucial to understand that saving alone is not the pathway to wealth. In order to achieve true prosperity, it is essential to complement saving with investment in passive income-generating assets. To illustrate this point, allow me to share the story of a lady who was a close friend of my mother.

This lady took frugality to an extreme level, exemplifying the notion of saving at all costs. She would recycle her dishwater, utilizing it repeatedly to wash her dishes. Furthermore, she adopted the practice of delaying lavatory flushing until after ten usages. While these examples may seem extraordinary (the latter certainly is), they serve as vivid illustrations of the limitations associated with the Penny Saver mindset. Individuals who adhere strictly to these extreme practices often find it challenging to truly flourish and experience a life of happiness and abundance.

It is essential to recognize that relying solely on a mindset of extreme saving will not lead to long-term wealth creation. Saving diligently is certainly commendable, and it can undoubtedly succeed in establishing a foundation of financial security with the potential to support our short-term monetary goals. To realize lasting prosperity, however, it is imperative to embrace the concept of investment and allocate resources towards passive income-generating assets.

Investing in passive income assets is key to unlocking the true potential of wealth accumulation. These assets may encompass various forms, including income-producing real estate, dividend-paying stocks, bonds, or even ventures that generate residual income. By diversifying one's portfolio and harnessing the power of compounding returns, individuals can foster sustainable wealth growth and open the doors to a life of greater financial freedom.

The lesson that should emerge is important: Striking a balance between saving and investing is paramount. While a dedication to saving every dime is commendable in theory, avoiding the pitfalls of an excessively restrictive mindset is crucial. By broadening our financial perspectives and embracing the potential of passive income, we can transcend the limitations imposed by an exclusive focus on saving. This shift in mindset enables us to seize opportunities, experience true prosperity, and build a life of abundance that extends beyond mere frugality.

THE *KEEPING UP WITH THE JONESES* MINDSET

There exists a phenomenon where individuals attempt to match the financial status of their neighbors by indulging in the purchase of lavish cars and expensive clothing that surpasses their means. This behavior stems from a place of jealousy, where one becomes envious of the possessions and accomplishments of their friends or family members, rather than finding genuine happiness in their success. Unfortunately, adopting such a mindset can swiftly lead to financial ruin that only serves to exacerbate this envy.

To combat this mindset, it is important to recognize that we should not concern ourselves with the extravagant spending habits of others, as we have no knowledge of their true financial circumstances. After all, perhaps they are keeping up with some Joneses of their own! Instead, we ought to focus on our own financial well-being and prioritize our own financial goals. Comparing ourselves to others and attempting to keep up with their possessions will only result in a rapid depletion of our resources, plunging us into a cycle that can be hard to rid of.

As I matured and gained wisdom through life experiences, I discovered the value of being genuinely happy for others. This is, perhaps, the purest remedy to 'keeping up with the Joneses' mindset. It is essential to cultivate a mindset of contentment and gratitude for the successes and achievements of those around us. Rather than allowing jealousy to consume us, we should celebrate the accomplishments of others and use their success stories as inspiration for our own journey towards financial stability and personal growth.

By shifting our perspective and redirecting our focus towards our own financial well-being, we can avoid the pitfalls of attempting to live beyond our means in order to match the perceived riches of others. True happiness and financial security come from within, not from the pursuit of material possessions or the comparison of our lifestyles to those around us. Embracing this mindset allows us to forge our own path and make informed decisions based on our unique circumstances, ultimately empowering us to forge a more fulfilling and prosperous life.

THE UNDER MATTRESS SAVING MINDSET

The "Under Mattress Saving Mindset" refers to individuals who harbor a distrust towards the financial system and, as a result, adopt unconventional methods to handle their finances. While they may choose to save their money by physically storing it under their mattress, they are unaware of the potential risks involved. Indeed, while your money may feel safe from the perceived threat of financial institutions, such an approach leaves your finances vulnerable to threats like fire, theft, and inflation. I once knew a pastor who had accumulated a significant amount of money from the weekly offerings of his congregation. He kept the funds in a plastic bag at his house, intending to use them for various church expenses. Tragically, his house caught fire, and this hard-earned money went up in smoke. Unfortunately, his homeowner insurance policy did not provide coverage for such incidents. Worryingly for the 'under the mattress saver', this is not uncommon; Homeowner insurance policies tend only to cover a limited amount of cash, usually a few hundred dollars, unless the specific amount has been declared to the insurance company in advance.

One common example of alternative saving methods is the traditional Sou-Sou. Originating in West Africa and the Caribbean, a Sou-Sou is an informal savings club that has been passed down through generations. Within a Sou-Sou, a trusted group of family and friends come together to participate in a savings arrangement. However, it is important to note that a Sou-Sou does not accrue interest or offer any protection against theft or inflation. This method is often utilized by communities with limited access to local banks, but it carries inherent risks and limitations.

An alternative strategy employed by individuals with a strong inclination towards saving is the utilization of prepaid debit cards. In this context, individuals choose to have their weekly earnings directly deposited onto a prepaid debit card. Nevertheless, it is imperative to consider that these debit cards frequently entail significant monthly charges deducted from the account, thereby potentially diminishing the overall capacity for saving.

While the intentions behind these alternative methods may vary, it is essential to understand that they may not all provide an equivalent level of financial security and benefits to traditional banking systems. Depositing money in insured financial institutions can safeguard against risks like theft, provide protection against inflation, help savers incur interest, and offer access to various financial services.

By gaining a deeper understanding of the advantages and disadvantages of different financial systems, individuals can make informed decisions about how to manage and protect their money. It is important to strike a balance between preserving trust in the financial system and exploring alternative options that align with personal beliefs and goals.

THE ADDICTED HABIT MINDSET

It is a widely discussed topic among financial gurus: when your habits drain you financially. Have you ever wondered how much money someone addicted to cigarettes must fork out to fund their habit, gradually impoverishing themselves while harming their physical health? Similarly, it is clear that a gambling addiction can lead to the rapid loss of a family fortune in a casino. Initially, items like cigarettes, alcohol, or drugs may seem like small expenses that fulfill an urge without significantly impacting your finances. Over time, however, the costs of these items can accumulate.

But let's not forget about the side effects. This does not refer only to the warnings listed on cigarette cartons, liquor bottles, or those commercials showing "your brain on drugs." Such effects are devastating, of course. For the purposes of this book, however, we are concerned with the financial and legal consequences of addiction, draining your pockets in the process. Health and financial effects can interact too, of course, with substance abuse oftentimes leading to expensive medical bills.

It is crucial to recognize the long-term financial implications of unhealthy habits and addictions. Not only do they deplete your financial resources, but they also bring forth legal and health-related challenges that further strain your finances. Breaking free from these destructive patterns is not only beneficial for your well-being but also for your financial stability. By prioritizing your health and making positive choices, you can avoid the financial pitfalls that often accompany addiction. Furthermore, your family shares the anguish alongside you, often feeling powerless as they witness their loved one struggling to win their battle with addiction. Each instance of a DUI arrest or substance overdose also takes a toll on the family. I have known individuals who have endured this harrowing experience. The family dynamic is forever altered, but finding solace by seeking appropriate professional assistance and allowing one's faith to guide the journey is possible.

CHAPTER TWO
INSURANCE

The purpose of insurance is to transfer the risk of potential losses from an individual or business over to an insurance company. For example, when a motorist with insurance suffers an automobile accident, the insurance company covers any liability for physical or property damage. Additionally, if the motorist's vehicle sustains physical damage, it may be covered under supplementary insurance such as comprehensive coverage. Various types of insurance are available, including auto, homeowner, life, health, disability, accidental, and long-term care insurance.

While certain forms of insurance are required by government regulations, many are optional. For example, insurance is oftentimes mandatory when registering an automobile or owning a mortgaged home. **Corporations** may also decide to take out life insurance policies on key employees, essentially ensuring that they can benefit financially if they lose their services to that employee. It is evident then, that companies value insurance highly. This reveals an important lesson: if major businesses believe that insurance is important. We as individuals ought to value it too! The recent implementation of universal healthcare in the US—branded Obamacare—has emerged as a response to hospitals facing financial strain. This pattern highlights the reality that insurance is often mandated when it benefits someone other than the individual, while optional insurance related to individual risk is left to personal discretion.

Personal Insurance

It is essential that our financial strategies prioritize the insurance that is not required by external entities. However, the availability of many insurance types can vary from person to person. I have had numerous people approach me for life insurance when they are, regrettably, no longer eligible due to age or health conditions. Indeed, qualification for life insurance depends on factors such as age, health, driving record, or occupation. Undesirable qualities in any of these categories can raise the cost of an insurance policy, or even render an individual ineligible for cover. Additionally, people often look for cheaper life insurance options and opt for term policies, which may be less expensive upfront but can end up costing more in the long run. Term insurance can be sensible in various scenarios, such as when an individual has a modest income or seeks coverage for a limited duration, typically less than 30 years.

Business Insurance

As an entrepreneur, it is essential to recognize the significance of business insurance in safeguarding various aspects of your company. Insurance plays a vital role in the formation and growth of a company, from protecting yourself and your employees to ensuring the well-being of your customers and the longevity of your assets. Consider the potential financial burdens associated with worker injuries, lawsuits, temporary closures, or data breaches. Without adequate coverage, any of these scenarios could pose a severe threat to the future viability of your business. Moreover, your state may mandate specific types of business insurance, further underscoring its importance.

Business insurance provides a safety net that shields you from unexpected costs and liabilities. The expenses arising from workplace injuries can quickly accumulate, including medical bills, lost wages, and potential legal actions. Appropriate workers' compensation coverage ensures your employees receive the support they need while protecting your business from significant financial strain. Lawsuits are another potential risk for which businesses ought to prepare. Whether related to contractual disagreements, product liability, or other matters, legal disputes can be expensive to defend against and may result in substantial damages for any company that finds itself on the receiving end of a verdict. Liability insurance is a crucial defense, covering legal costs and potential settlements or judgments, allowing you to focus on running your business rather than being overwhelmed by legal battles.

Temporary business closures due to unforeseen circumstances like natural disasters or fires can also devastate. Business interruption insurance covers lost income, ongoing expenses, and the costs associated with relocation or rebuilding. It ensures your business can recover swiftly and resume operations without suffering irreparable financial losses.

In today's increasingly digital age, new threats emerge in the form of data breaches and cyber-attacks. With an increasing reliance on technology, businesses must take proactive steps to protect sensitive customer information. Cyber liability insurance offers financial protection against the costs of data breaches, including legal expenses, notification to affected individuals, credit monitoring, and reputational damage control. Lastly, being aware of the insurance requirements specific to your state is crucial. Compliance with these regulations is not only legally mandated but also essential for the long-term success of your business. Failing to carry the necessary insurance coverage may result in penalties, fines, or even a suspension of your business operations.

By recognizing the multitude of risks that businesses face and understanding the significance of comprehensive insurance coverage, you can fortify your company's foundation and protect against future risks. Consult with insurance professionals to assess your unique needs and explore suitable policies that align with your industry and state requirements. Prioritizing business insurance demonstrates your commitment to mitigating potential threats and ensuring the continuity and prosperity of your venture.

WHY DO PEOPLE NEED INSURANCE?

One of the primary reasons why people need insurance is to protect against financial loss. Accidents and unexpected events can happen at any time and, without proper insurance, the cost of repairing or replacing property, covering medical expenses, or addressing legal claims can be prohibitively expensive. For example, suppose you are involved in a car accident at a time when you do not have any car insurance. As if the accident itself wasn't devastating enough, you could find yourself liable for thousands of dollars in damages. Insurance can also help to mitigate risk and uncertainty in life. By paying a relatively small amount in premiums, you can protect yourself against potentially devastating financial consequences that could arise from various situations. For example, life insurance can provide financial security for your family in the event of your unexpected death, or disability insurance can help replace lost income if you become disabled and unable to work. As mentioned above, insurance is often required by law. For example, auto insurance is mandatory in most states, and employers must carry workers' compensation insurance to protect their employees.

Another significant benefit of insurance is the peace of mind and sense of security it provides. Knowing that you are protected against unforeseen events can help reduce the stresses and anxieties surrounding our financial security, allowing you to focus on the things that matter most in life. Whether you are a business owner, a homeowner, or an individual looking to protect your family's financial future, insurance can provide the peace of mind you need to live your life confidently. Whether you are looking to protect your family's future, trade, or personal assets, insurance is an essential tool for achieving your goals and living your happiest, most successful life.

TYPES OF INSURANCE

There are several types of insurance available to individuals and businesses, with some of the most common including:

Auto Insurance

Auto insurance provides financial protection and peace of mind to individuals who own and operate motor vehicles. It serves as a safeguard against unexpected events, accidents, and potential liabilities that can arise while driving on public roads. Indeed, auto insurance is a legal requirement in many jurisdictions, a legality that ensures that individuals take financial responsibility for any damages or injuries they may cause while operating a vehicle. Auto insurance policies offer various coverage options, allowing customized coverage based on everyone's specific needs, preferences, and budget.

Liability coverage is a fundamental component of auto insurance and is typically required by law. It provides coverage for injuries or property damage caused to others in an accident for which the insured driver is deemed to be at fault. This helps protect the driver from the financial burden of potential lawsuits, medical expenses, and property repairs that may arise from an accident. In addition to liability coverage, individuals can choose to add comprehensive and collision coverage to their auto insurance policy. Comprehensive coverage protects against damage to the insured vehicle caused by non-collision events such as theft, vandalism, natural disasters, or falling objects. Collision coverage, as the name suggests, covers damages to the insured vehicle resulting from collisions with other vehicles, objects, or rollovers. Uninsured/underinsured motorist coverage stands as a vital component within the realm of auto insurance. This coverage serves to safeguard the insured driver and their passengers in the event of an accident involving a driver who lacks insurance or possesses inadequate coverage to fully address the resulting damage. By having uninsured/underinsured motorist coverage in place, the injured party is assured of receiving appropriate compensation for medical expenses, lost wages, and other damages, even if the responsible driver is incapable of providing it. Thus, this coverage ensures that individuals are adequately protected and fairly compensated despite the circumstances surrounding the at-fault driver's insurance situation. In addition, auto insurance policies may offer optional coverage such as medical payments coverage, which helps cover medical expenses for the insured driver and passengers, regardless of who is at fault in an accident. Rental reimbursement coverage, meanwhile, can assist with the cost of renting a replacement vehicle while the insured vehicle is being repaired after an accident.

When purchasing auto insurance, it is important to consider the policy limits and deductibles. The policy limit is the *maximum* amount that the insurance company will pay for a covered claim, while the deductible is the amount the insured individual must pay out of their own pocket before the insurance coverage applies. By selecting appropriate limits and deductibles, individuals can strike a balance between affordability and the level of protection they desire. To find the right auto insurance policy, it is beneficial to shop around, compare quotes from different insurance providers, and consider factors such as customer service, claims handling, and the insurer's financial stability. Experienced insurance agents can be contacted for valuable guidance when it comes to understanding the coverage options, policy terms, and discounts that are available for your personal set of circumstances.

By investing in auto insurance, individuals ensure that they are financially protected in the case of accidents, damage, or theft involving their vehicles. It not only helps cover the cost of repairs and medical expenses but also provides legal protection and peace of mind. Auto insurance serves as a responsible choice that promotes safety on the roads and protects individuals and their assets from unforeseen circumstances.

Homeowner's Insurance

Homeowner's insurance is crucial for safeguarding homeowners and their properties, providing financial security and peace of mind against unexpected events and risks. The main goal of homeowner's insurance is to lessen the financial impact of any losses or damages that might be sustained by a house or its contents. Homeowner's insurance provides protection from the financial obligations that might result from these bad circumstances, whether they are caused by natural disasters like fires, storms, or floods or human-related occurrences like theft, vandalism, or accidents.

Depending on the policy and the insurer, the coverage offered by homeowner's insurance can vary. To address different parts of safety, however, there are a few standard categories of coverage that are frequently included in homeowner's insurance policies. The fundamental component of these is dwelling coverage, which provides financial compensation for the upkeep or reconstruction of the physical structure of the house. This protection includes the foundation, walls, roof, and any affixed buildings like garages or sheds.

A second key component is personal property coverage, which covers home furnishings, technology, apparel, and other personal belongings. Up to the policy limits and subject to deductibles, this coverage reimburses the value of these possessions if they are lost, stolen, or damaged.

Another important facet of homeowner's insurance is liability protection. When someone is hurt on a homeowner's property and sues for damages, this serves to protect the homeowner. For homeowners facing liability claims, liability coverage can provide financial security and legal counsel by helping to cover medical costs, court costs, and potential settlements or judgements.

In addition, homeowner's insurance can provide extra coverage options to address requirements or dangers. These may encompass coverage for expensive objects like jewelry or works of art, protection against the results of natural calamities such as earthquakes or hurricanes, or coverage for occurrences including water damage or sewer backup. Homeowners should review their unique situation and the additional coverage alternatives available to make sure their policy sufficiently covers their needs.

It is crucial that we comprehend the policy's limitations, exclusions, and deductibles to guarantee that homeowners have the necessary coverage. For this, it is critical that we regularly evaluate and update the policy, particularly when making significant alterations to the house or purchasing new high-end belongings. Comparing prices from various insurers and speaking with an expert insurance agent are both recommended when purchasing homeowner's insurance. These experts can offer advice on choosing the best solutions for protection and assist homeowners in locating a policy that delivers through security at an affordable price.

By purchasing homeowner's insurance, people may safeguard their most asset and feel secure in the event of any unforeseen situations. After a covered loss or liability claim, this coverage acts as a safety net, guaranteeing that homeowners can reconstruct their life. This gives them and their family financial security and peace of mind.

Life Insurance

Life insurance is an essential kind of financial planning that provides individuals and their loved ones with financial security and peace of mind if the policyholder passes away before the policy takes effect. It is a contract between the policyholder and the insurance company, in which the policyholder agrees to pay recurring premiums to the company in exchange for a lump sum payment, also known as the death benefit, which would be paid out to selected beneficiaries upon the policyholder's death.

After the policyholder passes away, life insurance can give the policyholder's loved ones the financial support and stability they need to continue with their lives. This can involve covering immediate expenses, such as burial fees and existing bills, as well as providing long-term financial stability including the replacement of lost income, funding education expenses, or assuring the continuation of a business.

There exists a wide range of life insurance plans available for purchase, each offering distinct features and advantages tailored to meet the specific needs and goals of the policyholder. Among these options, term life insurance is a popular selection that provides policyholders with protection for a predetermined period, typically spanning from 10 to 30 years. During the active term of the policy, if the policyholder passes away, term life insurance offers a death benefit. Individuals often opt for term life insurance when they have heightened financial obligations, such as mortgage payments or raising their children.

An alternative is permanent life insurance, which offers coverage for the entirety of the policyholder's life as long (as the premiums are kept up to date.

Permanent life insurance policies, such as whole life and universal life insurance, not only provide beneficiaries with a death payment but also accumulate monetary value over time. This cash value is accessible during the lifetime of the policyholder and can be used to fund various ventures, such as supplementing the policyholder's income during retirement or providing funding in the event of an emergency.

Life insurance policies—and their premiums—are often personalized based on factors such as a policyholder's age, health, lifestyle, and financial situation. As such, the insurance company will usually require any applicant to submit to a medical examination or furnish extensive health information that will be used to perform a risk assessment. Moreover, it is essential to reevaluate the requirements for life insurance on a regular basis in order to ensure that the coverage remains sufficient as one's life experiences evolve. Events such as marriage, the birth of a child, or large financial commitments may be a reason to modify your coverage level or contemplate the addition of additional policies to accommodate your new needs.

Life insurance not only affords the policyholder financial security but also the peace of mind that comes from knowing that their loved ones will be provided for in the case of their untimely demise. It can offer support in sustaining financial stability and security for the future, as well as providing a safety net for use during times of need. If you are thinking about purchasing life insurance, you should seek advice from a licensed insurance agent who can evaluate your specific requirements and suggest coverage that would meet those needs.

Health Insurance

Health insurance plays a vital role in providing people with access to healthcare services and ensuring financial stability. Its primary purpose is to help individuals manage and reduce the costs associated with prescription medications, hospitalization, and preventive care. There are diverse health insurance plans available, each designed with unique features and coverage options to accommodate a wide range of healthcare needs.

The main goal of health insurance is to give people the resources to afford vital medical care without having to pay exorbitant sums of money. Health insurance is required in many nations and plans typically require a contract between the insured and the insurance provider, under which the insured agrees to pay recurring premiums in exchange for coverage. Depending on your policy and provider, the scope of health insurance coverage might vary greatly. Indeed, while a range of medical services, including doctor visits, hospital stays, prescription drugs, preventive care, and specialty treatments, are covered by some comprehensive insurance policies, others concentrate on a smaller range of medical services, or charge lower premiums but require higher out-of-pocket expenses.

Cost-sharing agreements are a common feature of health insurance coverage, where the insured person is accountable for covering a portion of their medical costs. Deductibles, co-payments, and co-insurance are a few examples of how people might share the cost of their medical care with their insurance provider. In order to ensure that the insurer can control risk while delivering essential benefits, health insurance policies may also contain annual or lifetime coverage restrictions.

Access to preventative care is a key advantage of health insurance. Routine examinations, immunizations, and screenings that might aid in identifying and addressing potential health issues before they become more serious or expensive to treat are frequently covered by health insurance policies. This focus on prevention encourages general health, and it may help with early detection and better chronic illness management.

Before choosing a health insurance plan, people should thoroughly research and compare all available options. Monthly rates, deductible levels, coverage caps, prescription drug benefits, and the network of healthcare providers are all things to think about, and you should weigh up how each option aligns with your personal situation. To ensure that particular healthcare requirements are appropriately covered, it is also crucial to understand the policy's exclusions and restrictions.

Disability Insurance

Some time ago, I attempted to offer my sister-in-law life and disability insurance. She somewhat dismissed my offer. I am unsure whether this rejection was due to our family connection, or because she simply did not acknowledge the value of the service I was offering. Sadly, it wasn't long before tragedy struck her. A few years later, she was involved in a car accident that resulted in a broken arm and leg. I was devastated by her injuries, but what pained me the most was witnessing her simultaneous financial difficulties and physical pain. She couldn't fully focus on her recovery because the burdens of rent and car payments weighed heavily on her mind. Had she taken out disability insurance, a huge weight would have been lifted.

Disability insurance is a valuable form of protection that offers individuals financial support and peace of mind in the face of unforeseen circumstances. While many people prioritize insuring their homes, vehicles, and health, disability insurance is often overlooked, despite its importance in safeguarding one's income and financial stability. Disability insurance provides income replacement in the event that a disability renders you unable to work. It ensures that you continue to receive a portion of your regular income, allowing you to meet your financial obligations and maintain your standard of living during a challenging time. It serves as a safety net, offering financial security and stability when you need it the most. It is important to note that disability insurance is not just for those in high-risk professions or physically demanding jobs; Whether you work in an office, a construction site, or a creative field, the risk of disability exists.

When selecting disability insurance, it is essential to understand the different types of coverage available. Short-term disability insurance typically provides benefits for a limited duration, often up to a year. Long-term disability insurance, on the other hand, offers coverage for an extended period, potentially until retirement age, depending on the policy terms. Some employers may offer disability insurance as part of their benefits package, while others may require individuals to seek coverage independently.

While the specifics of disability insurance policies may vary, it is crucial to carefully review and understand the terms, including the waiting period before benefits kick in, the duration of coverage, and the percentage of income replacement provided. Additionally, you should take note of exclusions or limitations within the policy to ensure that it aligns with your specific needs and circumstances. Think about the primary threats to your physical and mental health, and always ensure that these are covered by your chosen policy.

Liability Insurance

Imagine this scenario: You're hosting a backyard barbecue. The sun is shining, laughter fills the air, and everyone is having a great time. But, in a moment of clumsiness, one of your guests slips on a wet spot near your swimming pool and sustains an injury. Suddenly, your joyous gathering takes a serious turn, and you find yourself facing a potential lawsuit.

This is where liability insurance comes to your rescue. Whether you're a homeowner, a business owner, or even just an individual, liability insurance provides financial protection against legal claims and lawsuits due to bodily injury or property damage caused by your actions or accused negligence. It acts as a safety net, shielding you from the devastating financial consequences that can arise from unforeseen incidents.

For homeowners, liability insurance covers any incident that occurs on your property, such as slip and fall accidents, dog bites, or even damage caused by falling tree branches. It ensures that if someone is injured or their property is damaged while on your premises, you will not have to face hefty medical bills or legal fees on your own.

Business owners also rely on liability insurance to safeguard their operations. Whether you own a small shop or run a large corporation, accidents can happen at any time. A customer may slip on a wet floor, a faulty product may cause harm, or an employee may inadvertently cause property damage while on the job. With liability insurance, you can breathe easy knowing that if such incidents occur, your business assets and personal finances will be protected.

Of course, even individuals who are not property or business owners can benefit greatly from liability insurance. Suppose you accidentally cause a car accident that injures the other party and causes damage to their vehicle. Without liability insurance, you could be held personally liable for the medical expenses, vehicle repairs, and legal costs that subsequently arise. With the right coverage in place, however, you can rest assured in the knowledge that your insurance company will handle the financial aspects, allowing you to focus on resolving the situation on a more personal level.

When considering liability insurance, it is paramount that you consider your specific needs and the level of coverage that they require. Policy limits, deductibles, and exclusions can vary from policy to policy, so you must take some time to review your plan carefully and consult with an insurance professional to ensure you have adequate protection for your unique circumstances.

Remember, accidents happen. They are an inevitable part of life's journey. After all, you cannot control every outcome. Nevertheless, with liability insurance by your side, you can take on the world with confidence, knowing that you have a powerful ally protecting you from the financial consequences of unforeseen accidents and legal claims. So go ahead, embrace life's adventures, and let liability insurance be your trusted sidekick in the face of uncertainties!

Business Insurance

Business insurance is the fortress that shields your entrepreneurial dreams from the storms of uncertainty. When you pour your heart and soul into building a business, it becomes your lifeblood, your passion, and your legacy. But just as every great castle needs protective walls, your business needs the robust armor of insurance to withstand the unexpected challenges that may come its way. Think about the countless hours of hard work, the blood, sweat, and tears you have invested in your business. Your company is not just a job or a means to make money; it is a testament to your creativity, dedication, and vision. This is precisely why having the right business insurance is crucial: it acts as a safety net, ensuring that your dream will not crumble in the face of adversity.

Business insurance comprises a diverse array of coverage options meticulously designed to address the distinct requirements of various industries and operations. Its purpose is to safeguard your business assets, liabilities, employees, and reputation, thereby enabling you to concentrate on your core competencies—efficiently managing and expanding your business. Among the foundational forms of business insurance, general liability insurance assumes a prominent role. This robust shield of protection acts as a superhero, shielding your business from third-party claims pertaining to bodily injury, property damage, or advertising injury. Whether a customer slips and falls in your store, a product you sold causes a consumer some harm, or you inadvertently use someone else's copyrighted material, general liability insurance has your back.

But that is just the tip of the business insurance iceberg. Depending on the nature of your business, you may also need commercial property insurance to safeguard your physical assets, such as your building, equipment, inventory, and furniture, against perils like fire, theft, or natural disasters. This ensures that if your business premises are damaged or destroyed, you will avoid the devastating burden of needing to restart from scratch. For businesses with vehicles, commercial auto insurance steps in to protect your company's vehicles and drivers. Whether you have a fleet of delivery trucks, service vehicles, or simply use your personal car for business purposes, commercial auto insurance covers accidents, vehicle damage, and liability claims, giving you all-important peace of mind on the road.

Another critical aspect of business insurance is workers' compensation coverage. This superhero-like protection provides benefits to employees who suffer work-related injuries or illnesses. It not only takes care of medical expenses and lost wages but also shields your business from potential lawsuits arising from workplace accidents. But wait, there's more! Business insurance can also include professional liability insurance, also known as errors and omissions insurance, which shields professionals from claims of negligence or inadequate work. This is particularly crucial for businesses in fields like law, medicine, architecture, and consulting, where even the smallest of mistakes can result in significant financial consequences.

Business interruption insurance steps in when unexpected events, such as fires, natural disasters, or other perils, force your business to temporarily halt operations. It provides coverage for lost income, ongoing expenses, and even helps with the cost of relocating or setting up a temporary workspace, allowing you to get back on your feet quickly. Cyber liability insurance has become increasingly important in today's rapidly evolving digital age. With cyber threats lurking around every virtual corner, businesses face an unprecedented susceptibility to data breaches, ransomware attacks, and other cybercrimes.

Cyber liability insurance helps cover the costs of data recovery, legal fees, public relations efforts, and potential liability arising from such incidents. The world of business insurance is vast and complex, with numerous additional coverages available to address specific risks. Whether it's employment practices liability insurance, directors' and officers' insurance, or product liability insurance, you will be able to find—with a little bit of research—a policy tailored to meet the unique needs of your business.

Travel Insurance

Picture this: You have been planning your dream vacation for months, meticulously selecting the perfect destination, booking the best flights, and arranging the ideal accommodations. Everything seems flawless, until a family emergency requires you to cancel your trip. The emotional disappointment is bad enough, but might all your hard-earned money be lost too? This is where travel insurance takes to the stage, offering trip cancellation and interruption coverage. It reimburses you for non-refundable expenses and provides financial protection against unforeseen circumstances that force you to alter your plans.

But trip cancellation is just one potential hiccup that can be cured with travel insurance. Once you embark on your adventure, you want to have the freedom to fully immerse yourself in the experience, knowing that you are protected from unexpected mishaps or accidents. Travel insurance helps provide this peace of mind, covering medical expenses, emergency medical evaluations, and repatriation if you fall ill or incur any injury during your travels. From minor ailments to more serious medical emergencies, travel medical insurance ensures that you receive the necessary care without bearing the burden of exorbitant medical bills.

Now, let's not forget about those other travel mishaps that can put a dampener on your journey. Lost baggage, delayed flights, or stolen passports are unfortunate realities that travelers may encounter and can be particularly problematic for those embarking on short trips. Thankfully, travel insurance offers coverage for baggage loss, travel delays, and even assistance with passport replacement. With these protections in place, you can navigate through unexpected hurdles with ease, knowing that you are not alone in resolving these potentially problematic issues.

Adventure enthusiasts and thrill-seekers, listen up! If you are planning to engage in adrenaline-pumping activities like skydiving, bungee jumping, or scuba diving, you should ensure that you add adventure sports coverage to your travel insurance plan. This specialized add-on ensures that you are protected from injuries incurred while participating in high-risk activities, so you can push your limits and create lifelong memories with confidence. Without this add-on, any injury you suffer during such activities may not be covered.

But travel insurance is not just about physical protection—it also offers a safety net for your financial investments. Let's say you pre-paid for a luxury resort, but the company suddenly goes bankrupt before your arrival. Travel insurance can provide coverage for financial default, ensuring that you are not left empty-handed and allowing you to salvage your vacation plans.

Now, imagine finding yourself in a foreign country, faced with a medical emergency or a travel-related crisis. It's a daunting prospect, but with travel assistance services, help is just a phone call away. Travel insurance often includes 24/7 emergency assistance, providing you with access to a network of professionals who can offer guidance, coordinate medical services, or assist with language barriers. Think of these people as your personal travel guardians, ready to lend a helping hand when you need it most.

Travel insurance is a versatile shield that adapts to your unique travel needs. Whether you are a seasoned explorer, a globetrotting family, or a business traveler, you can always find a policy tailored to fit your requirements. From single-trip insurance to annual multi-trip policies, you can choose the coverage that aligns with your travel habits and preferences.

Professional Liability Insurance

Picture yourself as a skilled professional, extending your skills to clients and guiding them through intricate challenges. With unwavering confidence in your abilities and a well-documented history of triumphs, you find yourself confronted with an unexpected situation: a client alleges that your services have inflicted financial loss or harm upon them. Fear not, for professional liability insurance emerges as the heroic guardian of the professional realm, poised to shield you when your reputation and livelihood hang in the balance.

Professional liability insurance, also known as errors and omissions (E&O) insurance, is specifically designed for individuals and businesses in professional services industries. It provides protection against claims of negligence, errors, omissions, or inadequate work that result in financial loss for your clients. In effect, it is like always having an invisible legal time by your side, skilled and ready to focus on the intricacies of a lawsuit while you continue to focus on what you do best!

Let's say you are a consultant providing strategic advice to businesses. You've been working closely with a client for months, helping them navigate a challenging market landscape. Unfortunately, despite your best efforts, their business is taking a downturn, and the CEO blames you for the financial setback.

While the setback may not be your fault, a lengthy and expensive lawsuit could follow. With professional liability insurance, however, you are shielded from the potentially devastating costs of this legal defense and the potential damages that may follow.

What sets professional liability insurance apart from other plans is its tailored coverage for the unique risks' professionals face. Different industries have different standards, regulations, and potential areas of liability, and these requirements will be reflected in your personalized plan. Whether you are a consultant, architect, accountant, engineer, or any other professional, there is sure to be a professional liability insurance policy that aligns with your specific field of expertise. Your policy is a customized suit of armor that shields you from the arrows of uncertainty.

Of course, professional liability insurance not only protects your financial well-being but also safeguards your hard-earned reputation. In today's interconnected world, where information can travel the globe with a few clicks of a button, even a single negative review can tarnish your professional image. With the right insurance coverage, however, you have the confidence and ability to handle any such challenges that come your way, knowing that you have the support to prove your innocence and protect your good name.

But professional liability insurance is more than just a safety net during a crisis—it is a valuable asset that can enhance your professional standing and image. Clients and potential partners are increasingly savvy and look for professionals who take their responsibilities seriously. By having professional liability insurance, you demonstrate your commitment to excellence, risk management, and client satisfaction. It's a powerful differentiator that can give you a competitive edge in a crowded marketplace.

As professionals, we strive for perfection, but we're only human, and mistakes can happen. Professional liability insurance recognizes this reality and provides a safety valve for those rare instances when things don't go as planned. It's a symbol of accountability, transparency, and professionalism in an ever-evolving business landscape. With professional liability insurance, you can face each day with confidence, knowing that you have a reliable partner watching your back.

Long-term Care Insurance

Long-term care insurance plays a crucial role in holistic financial planning, offering individuals the reassurance and monetary safeguard necessary for their aging years. Tailored to address the considerable expenses related to long-term care services, this form of insurance mitigates the risk of depleting personal savings and assets.

Imagine reaching your golden years, where you have worked hard and diligently saved for retirement, only to face the possibility of needing long-term care due to a chronic illness, disability, or simply the natural effects of aging. Without the proper coverage, the expenses associated with this type of long-term care services can quickly accumulate and put a significant strain on your hard-earned finances.

Long-term care insurance serves as a safety net against these threats, ensuring that you have access to the necessary care and support without depleting your savings. It provides coverage that can assist policyholders with daily activities such as bathing, dressing, eating, and medication management. Depending on the plan, it can also cover services provided in various settings, including nursing homes, assisted living facilities, adult day care centers, or even in the comfort of your own home. Policies can be tailored to meet your specific needs and preferences, allowing you the freedom to select the duration of coverage, the amount of daily benefit, and any additional features you may require (an important example is inflation protection, which ensures that your coverage keeps pace with rising costs over time).

By having long-term care insurance in place, you not only protect yourself but also your loved ones. It alleviates the financial burden that could otherwise fall on your family members, allowing them to focus on providing emotional support rather than worrying about the cost of care. It grants you the freedom to make decisions about the type and location of care you receive, empowering you to maintain your independence and dignity even in times of ill health.

It's important to consider long-term care insurance well in advance, as most policies have certain eligibility requirements, such as age and health status. Waiting until you need long-term care may limit your options or result in higher premiums. By planning and securing a policy early, you can ensure that you are protected when the time comes. Take the time to explore your options, understand the different policies available, and consult with a knowledgeable insurance professional who can guide you through the process. By proactively planning for your future, you can enjoy the peace of mind that comes with knowing you have taken the necessary steps to protect yourself and your loved ones. Long-term care insurance is a wise investment that offers priceless benefits for a secure and fulfilling future.

INTERIM SUMMARY

In summary, insurance is of paramount importance in enabling individuals and businesses to transfer risk, maintain financial stability, and navigate the uncertainties of life. Insurance encourages responsible behavior, promotes economic growth, and contributes to social welfare. Without insurance, the impact of accidents, disasters, and unforeseen events would be far more severe. Embracing insurance is, therefore, a fundamental aspect of prudent risk management and ensuring a secure financial future.

To effectively use insurance to protect your assets and leave a legacy, assessing your unique circumstances, goals, and risks is essential. Work closely with an experienced insurance professional who can guide you in selecting the right policies, coverage amounts, and limits. Regularly review your insurance portfolio to ensure it aligns with your changing needs and protects your assets adequately. Remember, insurance is not solely about safeguarding your assets; it is about providing peace of mind and ensuring a legacy of financial security for your loved ones. By taking proactive steps to protect your assets and mitigate risks through insurance, you can leave a legacy that will impact the lives of those you cherish most.

BUSINESS INSURANCE

Allow me to share with you the experience of a friend of mine who once owned her own cleaning service. As her business grew, she encountered significant setbacks as a result of neglecting the need for proper worker compensation. After one of her employees suffered an injury at work, her attempts to cut costs and avoid taking out the necessary insurance proved fatal to her business. She inadvertently put her business at risk by neglecting to obtain worker-compensation insurance and, when her employee got injured, she was unable to provide the mandatory financial support for their medical expenses and lost wages. The consequences of this decision were severe, with the worker compensation board—responsible for overseeing such matters—levying fines against her business. Ultimately, these costs proved insurmountable, leading to the downfall of a business which had thrived for close to two decades.

My friend's tragic story highlights the importance of obtaining adequate insurance coverage for your business. While reducing costs by avoiding insurance premiums may be tempting for short-term profitability, the potential long-term consequences can be so devastating that your business can very quickly cease to exist at all. Without proper insurance, a single, unexpected incident can lead to financial ruin, legal ramifications, and the loss of a business built over many years. It is, of course, advisable to avoid this long-term pain in favor of short-term insurance payments.

To protect your business and its employees, it is crucial to research and understand the insurance requirements relevant to your industry. Consult with insurance professionals to determine the appropriate coverage for your specific needs. Worker compensation insurance is essential to safeguard against potential workplace injuries and their associated costs. By investing in the right insurance policies, you can mitigate risks, protect your employees, and ensure the long-term viability and survival of your business. Do not let the allure of short-term cost savings lead to irreversible consequences.

WHY DO I NEED BUSINESS INSURANCE COVERAGE?

As an entrepreneur, understanding the importance of business insurance is crucial for safeguarding different aspects of your company. Insurance plays a vital role in protecting not only yourself and your employees but also ensuring the well-being of your customers and the longevity of your assets. It's important to consider the potential financial burdens that can arise from worker injuries, lawsuits, temporary closures, or data breaches. Without sufficient coverage, any of these situations could seriously jeopardize the future viability of your business. Additionally, it is worth noting that specific types of business insurance may be required by your state, further emphasizing its significance.

Business Insurance

Business insurance shields you from unexpected costs and liabilities. The expenses arising from workplace injuries can quickly accumulate, including medical bills, lost wages, and potential legal actions. Having appropriate workers' compensation coverage ensures your employees receive the support they need while protecting your business from significant financial strain.

Liability Insurance

Lawsuits are another potential risk that businesses must be prepared for. Legal disputes, whether related to contractual disagreements, product liability, or other matters, can be expensive to defend against and may result in substantial damages. Liability insurance is a crucial defense, covering legal costs and potential settlements or judgments, allowing you to focus on running your business rather than being overwhelmed by legal battles.

Business Interruption Insurance

Temporary business closures due to unforeseen circumstances like natural disasters or fires can also devastate your financial health. Business interruption insurance covers lost income, ongoing expenses, and the costs associated with relocation or rebuilding. It ensures your business can recover swiftly and resume operations without suffering irreparable financial losses. In today's digital age, businesses must take proactive steps to protect sensitive customer information from cyber-attacks and data breaches. Cyber liability insurance offers financial protection against the costs of data breaches, including legal expenses, notification to affected individuals, credit monitoring, and reputational damage control.

State Requirements

Understanding the insurance requirements particular to your state is of utmost importance. Adhering to these regulations is not just a legal obligation but also vital for your business's sustained prosperity. Neglecting to maintain the appropriate insurance coverage could lead to penalties, fines, or even the suspension of your business activities. By acknowledging the various risks that businesses encounter and grasping the importance of comprehensive insurance, you can strengthen the fundamental framework of your company. Consult with insurance professionals to assess your unique needs and explore suitable policies that align with the requirements of your state and industry. Prioritizing business insurance demonstrates your commitment to mitigating potential threats and ensuring the continuity and prosperity of your venture.

TYPES OF BUSINESS INSURANCE PRODUCTS

1. Business Owner's policy

The Business Owner's Policy (BOP) is a comprehensive insurance package that combines essential coverages such as business liability, commercial property, business income, and equipment breakdown into a single, cost-effective solution. This versatile policy can be tailored to your business's requirements or offered as an available package suitable for various industries.

Within a standard BOP, several key coverages are typically included. These include:

✓ *Commercial property insurance* protects your physical assets, such as buildings, inventory, and equipment, against risks like fire, theft, or vandalism.

✓ *Business liability insurance* protects in the event of third-party claims for bodily injury, property damage, or advertising mistakes, helping to cover legal expenses and potential settlements.

✓ *Business income insurance* safeguards against income loss due to a covered peril, allowing your business to recover financially after a significant disruption, such as a fire or natural disaster.

✓ *Equipment breakdown insurance* covers repair or replacement costs if essential machinery or equipment breaks down unexpectedly.

The beauty of a BOP lies in its flexibility and customization to suit your business's unique needs and requirements. Depending on your industry, additional coverage can be added or customized to address specific risks you may face. Whether you operate in retail, hospitality, manufacturing, or any other sector, a BOP can be designed to provide comprehensive protection tailored to your business's distinct characteristics. By opting for a BOP, you gain the convenience of consolidated coverage, simplifying policy management and potentially reducing costs compared to purchasing separate policies. This bundled approach offers a streamlined solution that addresses multiple facets of your business's risk exposure.

In order to guarantee that you possess adequate coverage, it is imperative to collaborate with insurance experts who can evaluate the unique needs of your business and propose the suitable BOP or customize it according to your specific requirements. By securing a BOP, you can have peace of mind knowing that your business is protected against various risks, allowing you to focus on what matters most growing and operating your business with confidence.

1. Business liability

Business liability refers to the legal responsibility that a business or organization bears for any harm, injury, loss, or damage caused to individuals, property, or other businesses due to its actions or negligence. It is an essential aspect of the legal framework that governs business operations and aims to protect various stakeholders from potential risks and consequences arising from business activities.

Fully understanding business liability demands an awareness and consideration of numerous different types of liabilities, such as contractual liability, tort liability, product liability, and employer liability. Each of these categories encompasses distinct areas of potential risk and legal obligation, which are expanded upon below:

- **Contractual Liability:** Contractual liability arises from legally binding agreements or contracts between two or more parties. When a business fails to fulfill the obligations as specified in a contract, it can be held liable for any resulting losses or damages suffered by another party. This may include breaching contract terms, failing to deliver the agreed-upon service, or violating provisions within the agreement.

- **Tort Liability:** Tort liability refers to the legal responsibility a business has for any harm caused to individuals or property due to its actions, be they negligent or intentional. Tort law covers a plethora of wrongful acts, including negligence, intentional infliction of harm, defamation, trespassing, and more. If somebody suffers injuries or damage as a result of any business failing to exercise a reasonable level of care, the injured party may be eligible to file a 'tort claim'. In other words, they can seek compensation for their losses.

- **Product Liability:** Product liability relates to defects or hazards associated with a product manufactured, distributed, or sold by a business. When a defective product causes harm to a consumer (perhaps due to a sharp edge, faulty mechanism, or toxic ingredient), the injured party can hold the business in the supply chain responsible for their injuries. Product liability claims may be based on design defects, manufacturing defects, inadequate warnings or instructions, or marketing misrepresentations, and so an abundance of supply chain players may bear a share of the responsibility.

- **Employer Liability:** Employer liability refers to the legal responsibility a business has for the actions or behaviors of its employees within the scope of their employment. If an employee engages in wrongful acts or negligence while performing their job duties, the employer may be held liable for the resulting harm or damage caused to others. Employer liability extends to situations such as workplace accidents, discrimination, harassment, or misconduct.

Business liability is a crucial consideration for any organization, as failing to adequately address potential risks can create significant financial losses, reputation damage, and legal consequences. To mitigate business liability, companies often take proactive measures, such as:

- **Risk Assessment:** Performing a comprehensive risk assessment allows businesses to identify potential hazards, vulnerabilities, and areas of legal susceptibility. By understanding the risks associated with their operations, businesses can take therefore proactive steps to minimize them and implement appropriate risk management strategies. In many cases, these preventative steps are more effective than any action that can be taken after an incident occurs.

- **Compliance with Regulations:** Adhering to relevant laws and regulations is essential to mitigate liability. Businesses must stay up to date with the laws applicable to their industry, ensuring that they comply with standards related to product safety, employment practices, data protection, environmental regulations, and more.

- **Insurance Coverage:** Securing appropriate insurance coverage, such as general liability insurance, professional liability insurance, and product liability insurance, can provide financial protection in the event of a liability claim. Businesses should carefully review their insurance policies to ensure that they include adequate coverage for their specific risks and liabilities.

- **Implementing Safety Measures:** Taking proactive steps to ensure the safety of employees, customers, and the general public is crucial in reducing liability risks. This may involve maintaining a safe working environment, implementing proper security measures, providing adequate training, and regularly inspecting and maintaining equipment and premises.

- **Documentation and Record-Keeping:** Maintaining thorough and accurate documentation of business operations, transactions, contracts, and safety protocols can be instrumental in defending against liability claims. Proper record-keeping can help establish due diligence, compliance, and adherence to regulations, which may be critical in legal proceedings.

- **Seeking Legal Counsel:** Engaging with legal professionals who specialize in business law and liability can provide valuable guidance and support. They can assist businesses in understanding their legal obligations, drafting contracts, developing risk management strategies, and representing them in the event of a liability claim.

It is crucial to emphasize that a business's liability risks and obligations can differ significantly based on various factors, including industry, location, size, and operational nature. Consequently, it is essential for businesses to seek tai-

lored legal advice and stay updated on evolving legal developments to profi-
ciently handle their liability concerns and responsibilities. Remember to *always* do your research to determine which legal advisor can help you best!

1. Commercial property

Commercial property insurance offers essential and comprehensive protection for your business's physical assets. While this insurance of course safeguards the business's main building itself, its coverage will typically extend to
surrounding commercial property and the valuable assets within (such as furniture, equipment and inventory). Thus, a great deal of potential issues can
be aided by this insurance branch. By obtaining commercial property insurance, you can mitigate the financial risks associated with unforeseen, covered
events that may damage or destroy your commercial property, with such occurrences usually including fires, burst pipes, storm damage, or vandalism.
Commercial property insurance helps recoup the costs involved in rebuilding, repairing, or replacing the damaged property, ensuring minimal disruption to your business operations.

While there may be some variation between plans, commercial property insurance policies typically offer two primary methods for valuing the insured
property:

- **Replacement Cost Coverage:** This coverage option ensures that
  the insurance will pay for the expenses of rebuilding, repairing,
  or replacing your business's property to a good-as-new condition.
  Importantly, replacement cost coverage does *not* factor in
  depreciation, allowing you to restore your property without any
  deduction for the diminished value over time. This method
  therefore provides a comprehensive level of protection, enabling
  your business to recover swiftly and resume operations as soon as
  possible following the detrimental event.
- **Actual Cash Value Coverage:** Actual cash value coverage ensures
  that your business is reimbursed according to the depreciated value
  of the property that has been damaged or destroyed before the

incident took place. This type of coverage considers various factors like wear and tear, age, and obsolescence. Despite factoring in depreciation, this coverage option still compensates for the cost of replacing the property, considering its reduced value. Opting for actual cash value coverage can be financially advantageous at first since the premiums are typically lower compared to replacement cost coverage. However, note that the reimbursement may not fully cover the expenses of replacement, as it accounts for the pre-accident value of the property.

When choosing between these valuation methods, it is crucial to evaluate your business's specific needs, financial capabilities, and risk tolerance. Replacement cost coverage offers more comprehensive and robust protection, allowing you to rebuild and restore your property without the impact of depreciation. On the other hand, actual cash value coverage may be a more suitable option for businesses with budget constraints, as it considers the property's diminished value but may not provide full coverage for replacement costs. Again, it is advisable to consult with an insurance professional who can assess your specific needs and guide you through the insurance selection process.

1. Commercial auto

Commercial auto insurance plays a vital role in protecting the vehicles utilized by your business for its daily operations. Whether you rely on cars, trucks, vans, or a fleet of vehicles, this coverage ensures that your business is prepared for unforeseen circumstances on the road. Commercial auto insurance typically comprises three basic forms of coverage, each serving a specific purpose in mitigating risks and minimizing potential financial liabilities associated with vehicular accidents.

- **Auto Liability Coverage:** Auto liability coverage is the cornerstone of commercial auto insurance, providing crucial protection in situations where your company – or its employees – are responsible for an accident that results in damage to another person or their property. If such an unfortunate event does occur, auto liability coverage steps in to cover the associated medical expenses, legal costs, and potential settlements or judgments. This coverage ensures therefore that your business is shielded from the financial consequences of accidents and helps maintain your reputation by addressing the needs of affected parties promptly and fairly.

- **Collision and Comprehensive Coverage:** Collision and comprehensive coverage work together effectively to protect your business vehicles from physical damage and loss. When it comes to collision coverage, it assists in reimbursing the expenses involved in repairing or replacing your vehicles after a collision, regardless of who is at fault. Whether your vehicle collides with another car, a stationary object, or experiences an overturn, this coverage guarantees that the costs associated with restoring your vehicle to its pre-accident state are taken care of. On the other hand, comprehensive coverage safeguards your vehicles against incidents that are *not* caused by collisions, and instead relate to theft, vandalism, fire, natural disasters, and other unexpected events. With comprehensive coverage, you can have peace of mind knowing that your vehicles are shielded from a wide array of risks that go beyond so-called 'typical' accidents.

- **Uninsured and Underinsured Motorist Coverage:** Uninsured and underinsured motorist coverage provides a safety net when your business vehicles are involved in accidents caused by drivers who either lack insurance or carry a policy that does not hold adequate coverage. In such scenarios, uninsured and underinsured motorist coverage helps pay for vehicle repairs and medical expenses incurred due to injuries sustained by you, your employees, or passengers in your business's vehicles. By having uninsured and underinsured motorist coverage, you ensure that your business is not left financially vulnerable in situations where the responsible party lacks the necessary insurance to cover the damages. This coverage acts as a safeguard, allowing your business to recover costs that would otherwise burden your own resources.

By securing comprehensive commercial auto insurance, you protect your business's vehicles and financial interests from the uncertainties of the road. Assessing your business's specific needs, consulting with an experienced insurance professional, and tailoring the coverage to your operations are essential steps in ensuring optimal protection for your commercial vehicles and peace of mind for your business.

1. Workers' compensation

When one of your employees faces an occupational injury or illness, it is crucial to have proper safeguards in place. Workers' compensation insurance serves as a valuable resource in such situations, providing coverage for a range of expenses associated with the incident. This insurance can alleviate the financial burden on both the employee and the employer.

Workers' compensation insurance primarily focuses on three key areas: medical expenses, rehabilitation costs, and lost wages. In the unfortunate event that an employee sustains an injury or falls ill while on the job, workers' compensation can help cover their medical bills. From initial emergency room visits to ongoing treatments, medications and rehabilitation therapies, workers' compensation ensures that the necessary healthcare expenses are taken care of throughout the employee's immediate support and subsequent recovery journey. By supporting the employee's recovery process, workers' compensation insurance promotes their successful reintegration into the workforce.

Additionally, workers' compensation insurance plays a vital role in providing compensation to employees for the wages they lose while recovering from an injury or illness. When an employee is unable to work due to such circumstances, it can have a substantial impact on their finances. Workers' compensation steps in by offering a portion of their lost wages, assisting them in meeting their financial responsibilities and preserving stability during this difficult period. By offering wage replacement benefits, the insurance policy provides a safety net for employees, ensuring they can focus on their recovery without worrying about their financial well-being.

Tragically, some workplace incidents result in the loss of an employee's life. In such devastating circumstances—situations which, of course, every business owner strives to avoid—workers' compensation insurance can offer vital support to the employee's family. To be specific, policies can provide financial assistance to cover funeral expenses and ongoing support for the deceased employee's dependents. By easing the financial burden on the family, workers' compensation insurance provides some measure of security and stability during an incredibly difficult period. It is important to note that workers' compensation insurance is a legal requirement in most states, although specific policy standards may vary. Compliance with these regulations is crucial to protect both employees and employers. By maintaining adequate workers' compensation coverage, businesses demonstrate their commitment to the well-being of their workforce and fulfill their legal obligations.

Overall, workers' compensation insurance is an essential tool for businesses to protect their employees and mitigate the financial impact of occupational injuries or illnesses. By covering medical expenses, rehabilitation costs, lost wages, and even providing death benefits, this insurance safeguards the well-being of employees and their families. Compliance with workers' compensation requirements not only helps ensure legal compliance but also fosters a safe and supportive work environment.

1. Business income

Business income coverage provided by workers' compensation insurance is an invaluable resource for businesses facing unforeseen circumstances that result in temporary closures and financial disruptions. This coverage extends beyond the traditional scope of workers' compensation, offering financial protection in situations where a covered loss necessitates business closure.

One of the significant advantages of business income coverage is its ability to help cover payroll expenses during a temporary closure. When a covered loss, such as a natural disaster, fire, or other catastrophic event, forces your business to temporarily cease operations, your employees may face uncertainty and financial strain. Business income coverage steps in to alleviate this burden by providing funds to cover payroll, ensuring that your employees continue to receive their regular wages during the closure period. This not only helps maintain their financial stability but also fosters loyalty and morale, allowing for a smoother relationship when your business is ready to reopen.

Relocation expenses can also be addressed through business income coverage. In the event of a covered loss that requires your business to relocate temporarily or permanently, the costs associated with moving can be substantial. Business income coverage helps offset these expenses, providing financial support to facilitate a seamless transition.

Furthermore, business income coverage plays a vital role in replacing lost income resulting from a covered loss. When your business experiences a temporary closure due to a covered event, business income coverage steps in to reimburse you for the income you would have earned had the closure not occurred. This crucial financial support allows you to meet your financial obligations, maintain your business's stability, and protect your long-term viability.

It is important to review the specific terms of your workers' compensation insurance policy to understand the extent of coverage available to you. Different insurance providers offer varying levels of coverage, and each comes with their own specific requirements and limitations. Your insurance provider can provide you with the necessary guidance to ensure that you fully comprehend the coverage available and any additional options that may enhance your protection.

Finally, business income coverage provided by workers' compensation insurance goes beyond the traditional scope of workers' compensation. By covering payroll expenses, relocation costs, and replacing lost income during temporary closures, this coverage helps businesses navigate unexpected challenges and maintain financial stability. Understanding the full extent of your business income coverage and its advantages empowers you to make informed decisions, protect your employees, and secure the long-term success of your business.

1. Crime insurance

Crime insurance is a critical safeguard for your business, providing comprehensive coverage against various criminal activities, including burglary, robbery, forgery, computer fraud, and employee dishonesty. By investing in crime insurance, businesses can effectively mitigate the potential financial losses associated with such acts.

Perhaps above all else, burglary and robbery are events that can disrupt the operations of a business and yield substantial financial losses. Crime insurance offers coverage in such scenarios, providing financial assistance to repair damages caused by a break-in or to replace stolen property. This coverage ensures that businesses can recover quickly and resume normal operations without bearing the burden of financial impact.

Forgery and counterfeiting present additional risk of monetary losses, but crime insurance safeguards businesses by offering coverage for losses incurred due to forged or counterfeit documents, checks, or currency. Likewise, today's digital age has seen computer fraud become a prevalent threat. Cybercriminals exploit computer systems and network vulnerabilities, leading to unauthorized access, data breaches, and financial fraud. Thankfully, crime insurance has adjusted to these emerging risks, and policies now typically cover losses resulting from fraudulent online activities and cyberattacks. This coverage extends beyond monetary compensation and often includes access to tech experts who can assist with mitigating the effects of a cyber incident.

Employee dishonesty is an unfortunate reality that businesses must be prepared for. Despite robust hiring procedures, it is always possible that we place our trust in an employee who goes on to engage in dishonest acts such as theft, embezzlement, or misappropriation of funds. Crime insurance offers coverage for losses resulting from such dishonesty, providing financial protection against such acts committed by employees during their employment. To be specific, your coverage can help recover the financial losses incurred due to the fraudulent actions of their employees and ensure that the business's assets and reputation are safeguarded.

Remember, crime insurance coverage and its specific terms and conditions may vary among insurance providers. Consulting with an insurance agent or provider is crucial to fully understand the range available and any additional endorsements or options that may enhance the protection of your business. Understanding the full extent of crime insurance coverage and its benefits allows businesses to make informed decisions, effectively safeguard their assets, and protect their long-term success.

1. **Employment practices liability**

Employment practices liability insurance is a critical form of coverage that can protect businesses from the financial risks associated with employee-related lawsuits. This provides essential protection in cases where employees file claims alleging discrimination, wrongful termination, harassment, or other employment-related issues. By investing in employment practices liability insurance, businesses can safeguard their financial well-being and reputation in the face of potential legal challenges.

Businesses face significant repercussions, both financially and in terms of their reputation, when confronted with discrimination allegations. To safeguard against such risks, employment practices liability insurance provides coverage for situations involving employee claims of discrimination on grounds such as race, gender, age, religion, or disability. This coverage provides protection by assisting with legal defense costs and potential settlement or judgment expenses, allowing businesses to navigate discrimination claims without incurring significant financial losses.

Wrongful termination claims are another area of concern. Employees may file lawsuits alleging that they were terminated unlawfully. Often, such claims will be motivated by a desire for retaliation against dissatisfaction. Employment practices liability insurance helps businesses address these claims by providing coverage for legal defense costs and potential damages. This subsequently allows businesses to defend their decisions and mitigate the financial risks associated with wrongful termination claims.

Harassment claims, including sexual harassment, can have far-reaching consequences for businesses. Allegations of harassment can damage a company's reputation and result in substantial financial losses. Employment practices liability insurance offers protection by covering legal expenses incurred when defending against harassment claims and potential settlement or judgment costs. This coverage not only provides financial support but also demonstrates a commitment to maintaining a safe and respectful work environment.

Additionally, other employment-related issues like defamation, invasion of privacy, and wage and hour violations expose businesses to legal risks. Employment practices liability insurance helps navigate these situations by offering coverage for legal defense costs and potential financial damages. With this coverage, businesses can address various employment-related claims without compromising their financial stability.

It is essential for businesses to carefully review the terms and conditions of their employment practices liability insurance policy. Coverage limits, exclusions, and specific provisions may vary among insurance providers. Consulting with an insurance agent or provider is crucial to fully understand the coverage available and any additional endorsements or options that may enhance the protection for your business.

In summary, employment practices liability insurance is a vital component of risk management for businesses. By protecting against employee lawsuits alleging discrimination, wrongful termination, harassment, and other employment-related issues, this coverage ensures that businesses can effectively address legal challenges while safeguarding their financial stability and reputation. Understanding the full extent of employment practices liability insurance coverage and its benefits empowers businesses to make informed decisions, maintain a positive work environment, and protect their long-term success.

1. Cyber liability

Cyber liability insurance is an indispensable form of coverage that businesses should consider safeguarding themselves against the potentially devastating financial repercussions of a cyberattack or data breach. This insurance provides comprehensive protection by assisting businesses in recouping expenses incurred due to such incidents, including legal fees and expenses related to notifying affected customers, investigating the cause of the attack, and recovering lost data or repairing damaged technology systems.

When a cyberattack or data breach occurs, businesses often find themselves facing complex legal challenges. Cyber liability insurance offers coverage for legal fees incurred in defending against claims or lawsuits that may arise as a result of the incident. This coverage ensures that businesses have the necessary financial resources to obtain expert legal representation, navigate the legal complexities, and protect their interests during the aftermath of a cyberattack or data breach.

Informing customers about a data breach is not only a legal obligation but also an essential step in maintaining trust and transparency. Cyber liability insurance provides coverage for the expenses associated with notifying affected customers, including the costs of sending out notifications, setting up call centers, and providing credit monitoring services. This coverage helps businesses fulfill their responsibilities in a timely and comprehensive manner, demonstrating their commitment to customer protection and minimizing the potential damage to their reputation.

Investigating the cause of a cyberattack or data breach is crucial for understanding the scope of the incident and implementing appropriate measures to prevent similar occurrences from happening in the future. Cyber liability insurance can cover the expenses related to forensic investigations conducted by specialized cybersecurity firms. These investigations help identify vulnerabilities, assess the extent of the breach, and provide insights for enhancing security protocols. By supporting these investigations financially, this coverage enables businesses to proactively address the underlying causes of the incident and enhance their cybersecurity posture.

Recovering lost data and repairing damaged technology systems are often complex and costly endeavors. Cyber liability insurance offers coverage for expenses associated with data recovery efforts and repairing or replacing compromised technology infrastructure. This coverage ensures that businesses can promptly restore their operations, minimize downtime, and mitigate the financial impact of cyberattacks or data breaches.

It is important for businesses to carefully review the terms and conditions of their cyber liability insurance policy, as coverage limits, exclusions, and specific provisions may vary among insurance providers. Consulting with an insurance agent or provider is crucial to fully understand the coverage available and any additional endorsements or options that may enhance the protection for your business.

1. Errors and omissions (E&O)

Errors and omissions (E&O) insurance is a vital form of liability coverage designed to safeguard your business from potential lawsuits arising from alleged negligent acts, errors, or omissions. This specialized insurance policy provides financial protection by covering legal expenses, settlement costs, and damages if a client or customer claims they have suffered harm or financial losses due to your professional services.

The scope of E&O insurance extends beyond just protecting you as an individual, also offering coverage to any employees and subcontractors who may be involved in the provision of professional services on behalf of your business. By securing this insurance, you create a safety net that shields your business and its stakeholders from the potentially devastating consequences of litigation.

Professional service providers, including consultants, financial advisors, architects, engineers, real estate agents, and legal professionals, greatly benefit from having E&O insurance. It is especially vital for these professions due to the inherent risks they carry. Even the most diligent professionals are prone to errors or inadvertently leaving out vital information, which can result in financial losses or harm to clients.

If your client files a lawsuit alleging errors, negligence, or omissions on your part, E&O insurance can cover the legal costs associated with defending yourself and your business. In the unfortunate event that you are found liable, E&O insurance also covers any settlement or judgment amounts awarded to the plaintiff, up to the limits of your policy.

Obtaining E&O insurance brings numerous advantages to your business. Firstly, it cultivates trust and confidence among your clients, who recognize your proactive approach to risk management and safeguarding their interests. This can give you a competitive advantage in the market and bolster your reputation as a dependable and credible professional.

Moreover, E&O insurance grants your financial security and peace of mind. It serves as a safety net, guaranteeing that your business's assets and resources remain shielded in the event of unexpected legal claims. This helps alleviate the potential financial burden and safeguards against the risk of bankruptcy arising from the costs associated with legal defense and potential damages.

When obtaining E&O insurance, you must carefully assess the specific needs and risks of your business. Policies can vary in terms of coverage limits, exclusions, deductibles, and specific areas of expertise they cater to. Working with an experienced insurance agent or broker can help you navigate through the complexities of E&O insurance and ensure that you secure a policy tailored to your business's unique requirements.

1. Equipment breakdown

Equipment breakdown coverage provides essential, comprehensive protection against various types of equipment failures, including those relating to mechanical malfunctions, power surges, operator error, and other unforeseen circumstances. By securing this coverage, you safeguard your business from financial losses and operational disruptions caused by equipment breakdowns.

Equipment breakdown coverage goes beyond covering the expenses of repairing or replacing equipment. It also takes into account the wider consequences of equipment failures, such as decreased productivity, business interruption, and potential damage to other property or assets. This coverage is applicable to various types of equipment, including but not limited to:

- **Machinery and equipment:** This includes essential machinery used in manufacturing processes, such as boilers, compressors, pumps, generators, and production lines.
- **Electrical systems:** Coverage extends to electrical distribution panels, transformers, switchgear, and control systems, protecting against power surges and electrical malfunctions.
- **Heating, ventilation, and air conditioning (HVAC) systems:** HVAC equipment, such as chillers, air conditioners, boilers, and ventilation systems, is vital for maintaining comfortable and controlled environments in commercial and industrial settings.
- **Computer systems and telecommunications equipment:** This includes servers, routers, telephone systems, data centers, and related infrastructure, which are integral to the smooth operation of modern businesses.
- **Refrigeration and cooling systems:** Equipment used in food storage, refrigerated transportation, and other cold chain operations, including walk-in freezers, coolers, and refrigeration units, can be covered under this policy.
- **Medical and diagnostic equipment:** Essential medical devices, such as MRI machines, X-ray equipment, ultrasound machines, and diagnostic instruments, are critical assets in healthcare facilities and

can be protected against breakdowns.

When equipment breakdown occurs, substantial losses can follow. Aside from the core costs associated with repairing or replacing the affected equipment, additional expenses such as temporary rentals, expedited shipping, and overtime labor. Moreover, the resulting business interruption and lost productivity can have far-reaching consequences, including dissatisfied customers, missed deadlines, and potential reputational damage. Equipment breakdown coverage helps mitigate these risks by providing financial assistance to cover repair or replacement costs, business interruption expenses, and associated losses. Though variation is inevitable, it typically comprises the following elements:

- **Equipment repair or replacement:** The policy covers the cost of repairing or replacing damaged equipment due to covered perils, such as mechanical breakdowns or power surges.
- **Business interruption coverage:** This element reimburses the income lost and additional expenses incurred as a result of equipment breakdown, helping to offset the financial impact of interrupted operations.
- **Extra expenses:** In situations where immediate replacement or temporary equipment is required, the policy may cover the extra expenses incurred to mitigate business interruption and maintain continuity.
- **Spoilage or contamination coverage:** For businesses that rely on refrigeration or cooling systems, this coverage protects against losses caused by spoilage or contamination of perishable goods due to equipment breakdown.
- **Other associated costs:** The policy may also include coverage for expenses such as equipment inspections, testing, and diagnostics to identify and prevent potential breakdowns before they occur.

By investing in equipment breakdown coverage, businesses can proactively manage the risks associated with equipment failures. This coverage not only provides financial protection but also offers peace of mind, allowing you to focus on your core operations without worrying about the potential consequences of equipment breakdowns. Working with an experienced insurance professional can help you assess the specific needs of your business and secure a policy tailored to your unique requirements.

1. Umbrella insurance

Umbrella insurance serves as a vital safety net for businesses, offering additional protection beyond the limits of your primary liability policies. This type of policy acts as an umbrella, providing coverage when the costs of a claim surpass the limits of your existing liability insurance. In high-loss situations where substantial financial damages are involved, for instance, an umbrella policy can help safeguard your business from potentially devastating liability claims.

To better understand the significance of umbrella insurance, it is useful to consider its practicality in an applied setting: Envision a scenario where your business confronts a general liability claim arising from an accident that took place on your premises. The injured individual is taking legal action, seeking $1.5 million as compensation for damages incurred. However, your general liability policy only provides coverage up to $1 million. Consequently, in the absence of umbrella insurance, your business would be held accountable for the $500,000 difference between the claim amount and your policy's limit.

This is where the true value of an umbrella policy emerges. By having umbrella insurance in effect, it can step in to cover the remaining $500,000 that surpasses the limit of your general liability policy. As a result, your business would not bear the weight of paying the excess amount of its own funds. This protective measure shields your financial assets and preserves your business's overall financial stability.

Umbrella insurance is particularly useful in cases where substantial claims arise, such as those involving severe bodily injuries, property damage, or instances where multiple parties are affected. By providing an extra layer of liability protection, an umbrella policy helps bridge the gap and shields your business from potentially catastrophic financial losses.

Moreover, umbrella insurance offers coverage across numerous liability areas, including general liability, employer's liability, and commercial auto liability.

This comprehensive coverage extends beyond the primary policies you hold, providing an added safety net that protects your business from various liability risks. It is important to note that umbrella insurance does not replace your primary liability policies but supplements them. It kicks in when the underlying policies have reached their limits, ensuring that your business is adequately protected even in cases of significant claims. By securing an umbrella policy, you gain peace of mind knowing that your business is safeguarded against unforeseen liabilities that exceed the coverage limits of your primary insurance.

To determine the appropriate coverage for your business, it is crucial to assess your specific risks, consider the nature of your operations, and evaluate the potential financial impact of a significant liability claim. Working with an experienced insurance professional can help you understand your business's unique needs and secure an umbrella policy tailored to provide the necessary protection.

Overall, umbrella insurance is a critical component of risk management for businesses. By offering an additional layer of liability coverage beyond the limits of your primary policies, it ensures that your business is shielded from potentially devastating financial losses arising from high-cost claims. Invest in umbrella insurance to fortify your business's defenses and protect its long-term financial stability.

1. Inland marine

Inland marine insurance is a specialized form of coverage designed to protect various types of property while in transit. Contrary to its name, inland marine insurance does not solely pertain to marine-related risks, but rather encompasses a wide range of movable property exposures. Whether you are shipping goods by land, air, or water, this coverage protects your assets against potential damages or losses that may occur during transit. It provides coverage for both owned and non-owned property, including inventory, equipment, machinery, and supplies, while they are being transported from one location to another.

Furthermore, inland marine insurance goes beyond safeguarding against risks solely related to transportation. It offers coverage for valuable assets that may be temporarily situated away from your establishment. This encompasses esteemed artwork, specialized tools and equipment, computer systems and data, mobile medical equipment, and other valuable properties. Whether you are showcasing artwork at a gallery, engaging in off-site projects, or transporting equipment to a worksite, inland marine insurance ensures adequate coverage to minimize the risks associated with these portable assets.

In addition to physical loss or damage, inland marine insurance can also offer coverage for perils like theft, vandalism, and accidental breakage, safeguarding your property against these risks and allowing you to focus on your business operations. When obtaining inland marine insurance, it is essential to accurately evaluate the value and characteristics of the property being insured. This includes identifying the specific items, their values, and the transportation or off-premises locations where they will be covered. Working closely with an experienced insurance professional can help ensure that your coverage adequately addresses your unique needs and provides the necessary protection for your mobile assets. By securing inland marine insurance, you can safeguard your property against potential losses, damages, or theft, enabling your business to operate smoothly and efficiently, no matter where your assets may be located.

1. Accounts receivable

Accounts receivable insurance is a highly advantageous type of insurance that offers protection for your business against potential losses resulting from customers' failure to make payments and potential damage to your records of accounts receivable. This specialized insurance provides crucial financial security and reassurance, guaranteeing that your business can effectively overcome the obstacles associated with outstanding invoices and associated setbacks. The primary objective of accounts receivable insurance is to protect your business against the inherent risks posed by customer non-payment. Whether due to insolvency, bankruptcy, or other unforeseen circumstances, situations may arise in which customers are unable to fulfill their payment obligations. In such cases, accounts receivable insurance steps in to compensate your business for the outstanding amounts, reducing the impact of bad debts on your cash flow.

Furthermore, accounts receivable insurance covers the loss or damage to your records documenting the amounts owed by customers. This can be crucial in situations where physical or digital records are destroyed as a result of occurrences like fire, natural disaster, or cyber incident. By covering the cost of recreating or restoring these records, this insurance helps you maintain accurate accounting and streamline your financial processes.

In addition to this, accounts receivable insurance also offers valuable support in managing your credit risk and enhancing your business's financial stability. By providing coverage for a percentage of the insured receivables, this insurance encourages responsible credit practices and enables you to confidently extend credit terms to customers and pursue growth opportunities without the fear of crippling losses from non-payment.

You should also note that accounts receivable insurance typically covers a specified percentage of the insured receivables, known as the indemnity percentage. This percentage may vary based on your policy terms and the level of risk associated with your customers. Working closely with an experienced insurance professional can help you tailor the coverage to your business's specific needs and ensure that you have adequate protection that allows you to mitigate the uncertainties associated with customer payment defaults and protect your bottom line.

1. Builder's risk

A builder's risk insurance is an all-encompassing form of coverage meticulously crafted to protect your construction endeavors at every phase, commencing with the groundbreaking ceremony and extending until the ultimate completion. This specialized insurance assumes a vital role in alleviating the risks and uncertainties inherent in the construction sector, affording substantial financial security and tranquility throughout the entirety of the project. A primary function of builder's risk insurance is to protect the physical structure and materials involved in the construction project, covering against perils including fire, theft, vandalism, natural disasters, and accidental damage. Whether you are constructing a new building, or renovating existing structures, this coverage ensures that your project is shielded against unforeseen events that could potentially cause costly setbacks or delays.

In addition to protecting the physical aspects of the project, builder's risk insurance also covers the associated expenses and financial interests, including the cost of labor, materials, equipment, and permits, as well as the financial interests of lenders or stakeholders involved in the project. By providing coverage for these critical components, this insurance safeguards your investment and allows you to move forward knowing that your project is protected against financial losses.

Moreover, builder's risk insurance offers coverage throughout the construction timeline, from the initial groundbreaking to the completion of the project. This means that risks during different phases, such as excavation, foundation work, framing, and finishing, are all considered. This comprehensive coverage ensures that you are protected at every step, regardless of the specific challenges that may arise during the construction process.

A builder's risk insurance is temporary and project-specific, expiring when the project is completed or the property is occupied or sold. Collaborating with an experienced insurance professional is crucial to obtain appropriate coverage that meets the unique needs of the construction project. It is an essential part of risk management in the construction industry, providing comprehensive protection for the physical structure, materials, expenses, and financial interests. This insurance ensures that construction projects are safeguarded from unforeseen events and potential financial losses, instilling confidence throughout every phase of the project.

CHAPTER THREE

HOW TO MAKE MONEY AND ACHIEVE FINANCIAL SUCCESS

Before offering advice, I enjoy sharing experiences or anecdotes related to the topic at hand. As you will have seen, these oftentimes relate to the endeavors of my friends or family members. In this case, however, I believe it will be valuable for me to share my journey with you.

I have always been a proud, hard worker. During my stint as a school bus driver, I worked weekends repairing and building computers, teaching myself the skills necessary to navigate the evermore technological world. Even when I did not have two jobs, I would spend my free time studying and brainstorming new money-making ideas. Before my time as a school bus driver, I worked as a nighttime security guard in an abandoned building. Once things settled down, I delved into the Commercial Driver's License manual to pursue that path. My focus has always been on being the best version of myself, not competing with others. I wholeheartedly rejoiced in the accomplishments of others, confident that my turn would arrive if I maintained steadfastness. Countless triumphant entrepreneurs, film stars, and musicians exert boundless effort, constantly pushing their boundaries. Yet, they also grasp the significance of rejuvenation and nurturing their aspirations. Additionally, it is crucial to avoid excessive fixation on wealth that may lead to compromising one's values. Striving for excellence in every endeavor holds utmost importance, irrespective of monetary gains. Seek assistance when needed; Nobody can do everything on their own. It is for this reason that I so highly value connecting with honest and professional individuals through networking. Additionally, giving back is an integral part of the money-making process. Exchange your time for knowledge and your resources to help others. Consider this book, then, as a resource passed down from me to you.

There are various methods of generating income, and it is advisable to have multiple streams to provide financial stability and security. Within the realm of income, there exist seven distinct categories: earned income, business income, interest income, dividend income, rental income, capital gains, and royalty income. The act of diversifying one's income is of utmost importance to mitigate unforeseen circumstances that may emerge. Additionally, comprehending the differentiation between active and passive income holds significant significance. To illustrate this concept more clearly, let's consider the real estate industry.

Active income requires *active* participation (of course), either physically or mentally, to generate income. For instance, a real estate investor actively searches for investment properties, purchases them, oversees renovation and repairs, and manages the project.

On the other hand, passive income operates differently. Passive income investors have a more hands-off approach. For instance, the same real estate investor will likely delegate the responsibility of managing the project to professional property managers, who handle tasks related to the operation and maintenance of the property. This is an example of passive income or—put simply—income that requires minimal effort from the investor. Active income involves active participation in income-generating activities, while passive income requires less involvement, often relying on professionals to manage the investments.

THE IMPORTANCE OF UNDERSTANDING THE PRINCIPLES OF MAKING MONEY

Money is an essential aspect of our lives, influencing the choices we make, the opportunities we pursue, and the lifestyle we lead. While some may consider it a taboo subject, understanding the principles that sit at the heart of making money is crucial for anyone seeking financial success and independence. In this section, we will explore the importance of grasping these principles and how they can empower individuals to build a secure and prosperous future.

Financial Literacy: The Foundation of Success

Financial literacy is the cornerstone of making money work for you. Understanding concepts such as budgeting, saving, investing, and debt management allows individuals to make informed decisions about their finances. By acquiring this important knowledge, one can break free from the shackles of financial uncertainty and take back [control of their economic well-being.

Building Wealth and Security

The principles of making money provide a roadmap to building wealth and ensuring long-term financial security. By learning how to save and invest wisely, individuals can grow their wealth over time. This wealth accumulation not only offers a safety net during emergencies but also opens up opportunities for personal growth, retirement planning, and even philanthropy.

Embracing Entrepreneurship and Innovation

Understanding the principles of making money goes beyond personal finance; it paves the way for entrepreneurship and innovation. Entrepreneurs who comprehend the dynamics of market demand, financial management, and risk assessment have a greater chance of turning their ideas into profitable ventures. By studying successful business models and learning from past failures, aspiring entrepreneurs can navigate the intricacies of the marketplace and increase their chances of financial success.

Freedom and Independence

Money, when managed wisely, offers the freedom and independence that we all inherently desire. The principles of making money empower individuals to break free from the constraints of financial limitations. Whether it is pursuing your dream career, traveling the world, or supporting causes you care about, a solid understanding of money principles allows you to make choices that align with your aspirations and values.

Navigating Economic Challenges

Throughout life, we inevitably encounter economic challenges such as recessions, job loss, or unexpected expenses. Understanding the principles of making money equips individuals with resilience and adaptability to navigate these turbulent times. By possessing a solid financial foundation, individuals can weather storms, identify alternative income sources, and bounce back from setbacks more effectively.

Leaving a Legacy

The principles of making money extend beyond one's lifetime. When wealth is accumulated responsibly and ethically, it can be leveraged to create a legacy. Through comprehension of philanthropic principles, estate planning, and intergenerational wealth transfer, individuals can guarantee that the fruits of their labor continue to generate a positive influence for future generations.

THE POWER OF SETTING FINANCIAL GOALS

In the pursuit of financial success and security, setting clear and meaningful financial goals acts as a guiding compass, illuminating the path to prosperity. Regardless of whether your dreams involve acquiring a residence, launching a business, or attaining early retirement, establishing financial goals serves as a catalyst for a prosperous future. This captivating piece of content delves into the profound impact of setting financial goals and how it empowers individuals to transform their aspirations into tangible realities.

Clarity and Focus

By establishing financial goals, you gain a lucid perspective on your desired achievements. It aids in delineating your financial priorities, enabling you to differentiate between short-term cravings and long-term objectives. By homing in on specific goals, you can channel your energy, time, and resources towards actions that align with your financial aspirations. Clarity and focus become your allies in the pursuit of financial success and will get you to your goal in the quickest possible time.

Motivation and Accountability

Financial goals serve as powerful motivators, propelling you forward on your financial journey. They instill a sense of true purpose and determination. When faced with challenges or temptations to stray off course, your goals act as reminders of the bigger picture and the rewards that await you. Moreover, setting goals holds you accountable for your financial decisions and actions, fostering discipline and resilience that can benefit us in all aspects of our lives.

Measurable Progress

One of the remarkable aspects of setting financial goals is the ability to track your progress. By breaking down your goals into smaller milestones, you can measure your advancement and celebrate achievements along the way. Seeing tangible progress boosts your confidence and reinforces the belief that you are on the right track. It fuels a positive feedback loop, propelling you towards even greater success.

Empowerment and Financial Independence

Setting financial goals empowers you to take control of your financial destiny. It liberates you from the grip of financial uncertainty and passivity, enabling you to proactively shape your financial future. By defining your goals, you become an active participant in the wealth-building process. With each milestone reached, you inch closer to financial independence, where your money works for you rather than the other way around.

Adaptability and Flexibility

Financial goals are not set in stone. Life is dynamic, and circumstances change. Setting goals allows for adaptability and flexibility along your financial journey. As you progress and encounter new opportunities or challenges, you can adjust your goals to reflect your evolving needs and aspirations. This flexibility ensures that your financial journey aligns neatly with your values and current life circumstances.

UNDERSTANDING DIFFERENT INCOME SOURCES

In the complex landscape of personal finance, understanding the various income sources is a fundamental step toward achieving financial stability and independence. By comprehending the intricacies of different income streams, individuals are empowered to diversify their earnings, maximize their potential, and build a solid foundation for a prosperous future. This comprehensive exploration delves deeply into the diverse world of income sources, equipping you with the knowledge needed to navigate the path toward financial freedom.

Earned Income

Earned income, often referred to as active income, is the most common income source for individuals. It encompasses wages, salaries, and tips earned through employment or self-employment. Such income is the direct exchange of one's time, skills, and expertise for financial compensation. While earned provides an immediate financial boost, it is subject to limitations regarding the number of hours worked and the availability of opportunities for advancement.

Passive Income

Passive income represents earnings generated with minimal effort or direct involvement. True financial freedom lies in a realm where money becomes your ally, working on your behalf instead of the other way around. Passive income streams encompass various sources, such as rental income derived from real estate properties, dividends yielded by stocks and investments, interest accumulated from savings accounts or bonds, and royalties earned from creative works or intellectual property. By leveraging assets and investments, individuals can create sustainable, long-term income that continues to grow even when they are not actively working.

Portfolio Income

Portfolio income is derived from investments in financial instruments such as stocks, bonds, mutual funds, and real estate investment trusts (REITs). It primarily includes capital gains from the sale of investments at a profit and interest income earned from bonds or savings accounts. Portfolio income offers the potential for substantial growth and wealth accumulation, but also comes with inherent risks and market fluctuations. Building a diverse investment portfolio can help mitigate these risks and provide a steady stream of income.

Business Income
Business income is generated through entrepreneurial endeavors and self-employment. It encompasses profits earned from running a business, selling products or services, consulting fees, or income from online ventures. Business income offers the opportunity for unlimited earning potential and the ability to scale and expand operations. However, it also involves risks and responsibilities associated with business management, including overhead costs, marketing, and customer acquisition.

Rental Income
Rental income is derived from leasing or renting out properties such as residential or commercial spaces. Real estate investments can provide a consistent stream of income through rental payments, potential property appreciation, and tax benefits. However, remember that this source of income does require careful management, maintenance, and understanding of the local real estate market. In other words, it is not necessarily a low-effort route to wealth.

Side Hustles and Gig Economy
Within the ever-changing work landscape of today's connected world, side hustle and the gig economy have emerged as prominent factors. Side hustles entail part-time jobs or entrepreneurial endeavors pursued alongside full-time employment, offering an additional avenue for generating income. On the other hand, the gig economy encompasses freelancing, contract work, or engaging in short-term projects facilitated by online platforms. These side hustles and gig economy opportunities allow individuals to monetize their skills, talents, and passions, offering flexibility, autonomy, and potential income diversification, and are becoming an increasingly popular route to income.

BUILDING MULTIPLE STREAMS OF INCOME

Nowadays, relying solely on a single source of income is no longer sufficient to achieve financial stability and create lasting wealth. The notion of constructing multiple streams of income has emerged as a potent strategy for diversifying earnings, diminishing dependence on a single source, and unlocking a realm of financial resilience and abundance. This extensive examination delves profoundly into the advantages, tactics, and prospective income streams associated with building multiple streams of income.

1. Why Build Multiple Streams of Income

● **Diversification:** Building multiple streams of income helps diversify your earnings, spreading your financial risk across different sources. This ensures that if one stream falters or faces challenges, you can still rely on other sources to boost your wallet.

● **Increased Income Potential:** By creating multiple income streams, you open the doors to increased earning potential. Each income stream adds to your overall cash flow, enabling you to generate more revenue and increase your savings and investment capabilities. This paves the way for long-term wealth creation and financial freedom.

● **Financial Resilience:** Having multiple streams of income provides a safety net during unexpected events, such as job loss or economic downturns. It safeguards against a complete loss of income and offers greater financial resilience in weather challenging times.

● **Flexibility and Freedom:** Embracing multiple streams of income grants you the flexibility and freedom to effectively manage your finances. It empowers you to explore diverse interests, embark on entrepreneurial ventures, and allocate your time and resources to activities that resonate with your passions and values.

This multifaceted approach opens avenues for personal growth and fulfillment while enhancing your financial stability. This enhances your overall work-life balance and sense of fulfillment.

1. Strategies for Building Multiple Streams of Income

• **Identify Your Skills and Assets:** Start by identifying your skills, talents, and assets that can be leveraged to generate income. While these will vary from person to person, they might include specialized knowledge, creative talents, or physical assets such as property or vehicles. Understanding your unique strengths lays the foundation for identifying income opportunities.

• **Explore Side Hustles and Freelancing:** Engaging inside hustles or freelancing roles empowers you to monetize your skills and talents outside of your primary job. This could involve offering consulting services, freelancing in your area of expertise, or turning a hobby into a profitable venture.

• **Invest in Income-Producing Assets:** Consider investing in income-generating assets such as rental properties, dividend-paying stocks, or bonds. These assets can provide regular cash flow and may even appreciate over time.

• **Start an Online Business:** The internet presents an extensive range of opportunities to initiate an online business. Whether it involves e-commerce, affiliate marketing, or digital products and services, establishing an online business can yield passive income and provide access to a global audience. This digital landscape offers the potential for entrepreneurship, scalability, and the ability to create a sustainable business model with a truly worldwide reach.

• **Develop Passive Income Streams:** Passive income streams, such as royalties from creative works, interest from investments, or income from automated online businesses, allow you to earn money with minimal active effort. Building passive income streams gradually frees up your time and creates a steady flow of income.

1. Potential Income Streams

● **Rental Income:** Owning and renting out real estate properties can provide a consistent and reliable stream of income.

● **Dividend Income:** Investing in dividend-paying stocks allows you to earn regular income based on the company's profits.

● **Royalties and Licensing:** If you possess creative talents or intellectual property, you can earn royalties or license your work for recurring income.

● **Online Business:** Establishing an online business, such as e-commerce, affiliate marketing, or content creation, offers a scalable and potentially passive income stream.

● **Investments and Portfolio Income:** Diversifying your investment portfolio with stocks, bonds, mutual funds, or index funds can generate income through dividends, interest, or capital gains.

BUILDING DIFFERENT CASH FLOWS ASSETS BY USING INVESTMENTS AND BUYING REAL ESTATE

Building different cash flow assets through investments and real estate can be a transformative strategy for creating wealth and financial security. By diversifying your portfolio and tapping into the potential of these asset classes, you can generate multiple income streams and build a foundation for your long-term financial success. Let's explore the various avenues for building cash flow assets through investments and real estate.

- **Stocks and Bonds:** Investing in stocks and bonds can be a powerful way to build cash flow assets. Dividend-paying stocks provide a regular income stream through dividend payments, while bonds offer fixed interest payments. By carefully selecting a diversified portfolio of stocks and bonds, you can create a consistent income stream from your investment portfolio.

- **Real Estate Rental Properties:** Investing in real estate, particularly rental properties, can be an excellent cash flow generator. By purchasing properties and renting them out to tenants, you can earn monthly rental income that exceeds your expenses, such as mortgage payments, property taxes, and maintenance costs. Even more impressively, real estate investments have the potential to appreciate over time, allowing you to benefit from both rental income and capital appreciation.

- **Real Estate Investment Trusts (REITs):** REITs are investment vehicles that pool funds from multiple investors to invest in income-generating real estate properties. Investing in REITs offers an opportunity to participate in real estate ownership without the challenges of direct property management. REITs often distribute a significant portion of their income to shareholders through dividends, providing a consistent cash flow.

- **Peer-to-Peer Lending:** Peer-to-peer lending platforms connect borrowers with individual lenders. You can earn interest on your loan investments by lending money to individuals or businesses through these platforms. Peer-to-peer lending provides an alternative to traditional banking channels and offers the potential for attractive returns and regular cash flow.

- **Dividend-Paying Funds:** Investing in dividend-focused funds, such as dividend mutual funds or exchange-traded funds (ETFs), can be a passive way to generate cash flow. These funds consist of a portfolio of stocks that pay dividends, allowing you to benefit from regular income distributions while taking advantage of diversification and professional management.

- **Royalties and Intellectual Property:** If you have creative or intellectual assets, such as patents, copyrights, or music royalties, they can become valuable cash flow assets. Licensing your intellectual property or receiving royalties for its use can provide a steady income stream.

In the pursuit of building cash flow assets through investments and real estate, the significance of diligent research, meticulous due diligence, and seeking expert guidance cannot be overstated. It is imperative to formulate a well-defined and informed investment strategy, considering individual risk tolerance, while also diversifying holdings to minimize potential risks. By consistently monitoring investments, reevaluating portfolios, and making necessary adjustments, one can optimize the potential for cash flow generation.
Building cash flow assets through investments and real estate requires long-term perspective, patience, and discipline. It is important to understand that returns may vary, and that risks are associated with each investment avenue. By carefully managing your investments, staying informed about market trends, and adapting to changing economic conditions, you can build a robust and diversified portfolio of cash flow assets that support your financial goals and pave the way for a prosperous future.

CHAPTER FOUR

TAX

In 2021, my 16-year-old son and 12-year-old daughter embarked on a joint t-shirt design company, a mission that marked their first foray into the world of entrepreneurship. Naturally, I took it upon myself to educate them about the tax aspects associated with running a business. One day, my daughter approached me with an amusing question, "Do I have to pay tax on my profit? I'm not sure if I want to be a business owner." This statement brought back memories because, throughout my 17-year career as an accountant, I had often heard similar queries from my clients.

These are a few of the frequently asked questions I come across often: "Is it possible to avoid paying taxes completely?", "Is it permissible to include my primary residence's water bill as a deduction?", "Can I deduct the rent for my residence?", "Are dog food expenses eligible for claiming as deductions?", or "Is it allowable to deduct money sent to my family in another country?"

The answers to such questions vary from situation to situation, of course. Yet a general theme emerges: many people harbor misconceptions about the reasons for filing tax returns and paying income tax. To shed some light on this matter, let me provide a brief history of the income tax system. Income tax was first introduced into the U.S. in 1862, when President Lincoln sought means to finance the expenses of the Civil War. Prior to the implementation of income tax, tariffs were imposed on imported goods, and excise taxes were levied on specific items such as fuel and airline tickets, which served as revenue sources for the government. As the government expanded and required more funding, however, they realized that a more complex tax system was needed to accommodate the needs of federal, state, and local governments.

The tax revenues we provide serve a wide range of purposes. They support critical services such as our military, government agencies, road maintenance, police and fire departments, schools, and public hospitals. These funds play a crucial role in maintaining the infrastructure and institutions that ensure the efficient functioning of our society. Understanding the rationale behind taxes and their allocation can help dispel misconceptions and foster a greater appreciation for the role they play in supporting public goods and services. This, then, will be the focus of our fourth chapter.

THE HISTORY AND DEFINITION OF TAX

Tax is a compulsory financial contribution levied by a government or other authority on income, goods, or services as a means of funding public services and infrastructure. In modern society, tax is a fundamental concept in economics and finance, playing a vital role in shaping the functioning of the world that surrounds us. Taxes operate at several levels—indeed, they can be imposed on individuals, businesses, and other entities—and are likewise collected by governments at various levels, such as federal, state, or local.

Taxation is a longstanding concept, dating back to ancient civilizations like Rome, Greece, and Egypt, where records show the imposition of taxes. However, the modern notion of taxation, as we now understand it, developed during the emergence of nation-states in Europe between the 16th and 17th centuries. With the growth of centralized government, taxation became an essential tool for funding wars, maintaining social order, and providing public services. In modern times, taxes fund public services such as healthcare, education, defense, transportation, and social welfare programs. Moreover, taxes can also be used to promote social and economic objectives, such as reducing income inequality or incentivizing certain behaviors.

There are different categories of taxes imposed on different entities. One of the most prevalent types is income tax, which is imposed on the earnings of individuals and businesses. Sales tax is another kind of tax that is levied on the purchase of goods and services. Property tax pertains to taxes on real estate and other forms of property, while corporate tax refers to taxes on the profits of corporations. Excise tax is imposed on specific goods and services, such as alcohol, tobacco, and gasoline. Lastly, estate tax, also known as inheritance tax, is a tax on an individual's assets following their demise.

Tax calculations are based on various factors, including the income one earns, the assets they own, and the type of tax being levied. Marginal tax rates are used to determine the tax rate for different income brackets, while deductions and exemptions can reduce the amount of taxable income. Tax credits are used to reduce the amount of tax owed, while withholding taxes are deducted from an individual's paycheck before it is received.

PURPOSE OF TAXATION

The purpose of taxation is multifaceted, and governments aim to achieve an assortment of objectives through the imposition of taxes. Generally speaking, the primary purpose of taxation is to raise revenue to fund public goods and services that benefit society as a whole. However, taxation can also promote social and economic objectives, such as reducing income inequality, incentivizing certain behaviors, and stabilizing the economy.

One of the primary purposes of taxation is to raise revenue to finance the functioning of the government and provide public goods and services. This includes funding for essential services such as healthcare, education, infrastructure, national defense, and social welfare programs. Taxes play a crucial role in enabling governments to provide services that would otherwise be unaffordable for individuals to bear the costs of independently.

In addition to raising revenue, taxation is frequently used to promote social and economic objectives. For example, progressive income taxes can redistribute wealth from high-income earners to low-income earners, thus promoting social justice and reducing poverty. Similarly, taxes on tobacco and alcohol can discourage unhealthy behaviors, while other tax incentives can encourage desirable behaviors such as investing in renewable energy or making charitable donations.

Taxation serves another significant purpose of stabilizing the economy and fostering economic growth. Tax policies can be employed to influence economic activities by offering incentives for investment, consumption, and entrepreneurship. For instance, reducing corporate tax rates can motivate businesses to invest in new equipment, expand their operations, and generate employment opportunities, thereby stimulating economic growth. Further, tax credits for research and development can encourage innovation and stimulate economic activity.

Overall, the purpose of taxation is to raise revenue to fund public goods and services while also promoting social and economic objectives. While taxes can be controversial and unpopular, they are essential for the functioning of government and the provision of public goods and services, and effective tax policy can promote economic growth, reduce income inequality, and improve the well-being of society.

TYPES OF TAX

INCOME TAX

Income tax is a tax levied on the income earned by individuals, businesses, and other entities. It is a direct tax that is collected by the government to fund public services and programs. In most countries, income tax is the primary source of revenue for the government. The concept of income tax dates to ancient times when rulers would collect a portion of the crops or livestock from their subjects as a form of tax. Over time, income tax evolved to become a more sophisticated form of taxation that is based on an individual's or business's income.

Income tax is calculated based on the taxpayer's income, which can include wages, salaries, bonuses, rental income, investment income, and other forms of income. The tax rate is usually progressive, meaning that the more income an individual earns, the higher the tax rate they pay. Governments utilize income tax revenue to finance a diverse range of public services, including healthcare, education, infrastructure, and social welfare programs. Income tax also plays a role in diminishing income inequality by redistributing wealth from individuals with higher incomes to those with lower incomes.

In most nations around the world, income tax is collected through a system of withholding tax. That is, employers actively withhold a portion of their employees' income and remit it to the government on their behalf. Thus, most individuals never see the money that gets paid toward income taxation on their behalf. This is different for people who are self-employed or have additional sources of income, however. Such people are required to file an income tax return themselves and, once the government calculates the amount owed, pay the appropriate amount of tax direct from their bank account. The complexity of income tax regulations can make it challenging for individuals and businesses to navigate. Taxpayers—especially the self-employed—must keep accurate records of their income and expenses, understand the tax laws and regulations, and file their tax returns accurately and on time. Failure to comply with income tax regulations can result in penalties and fines.

Governments regularly review and update their income tax laws and regulations to ensure that they are fair, effective, and efficient. They also provide incentives such as tax credits, deductions, and exemptions to encourage certain behaviors, such as charitable giving or investment in specific industries. Remember, income tax, however frustrating it can seem, serves as a vital revenue source for governments worldwide. It is a direct tax imposed on individuals and businesses, calculated based on their income. Income tax plays a significant role in financing public services and programs, addressing income inequality, and supporting social welfare initiatives. However, navigating the complex regulations surrounding income tax can be challenging, and taxpayers must comply with the laws and regulations to avoid penalties and fines.

SALES TAX

Sales tax is a form of tax that is collected on the sale of goods and services. It is an indirect tax that the consumer pays when they purchase a product or service. The sales tax rate varies from country to country and even within different regions of the same country. The concept of sales tax dates to ancient times when traders and merchants would pay a portion of their sales as a form of tax to the ruling authority. Today, sales tax is one of the most common forms of taxation used by governments to generate revenue.

In the majority of countries, sales tax is collected by the retailer at the point of sale and subsequently submitted to the government at regular intervals. The tax rate typically represents a percentage of the product or service's sale price and may vary depending on the specific type of product or service being sold. Once in the hands of the government, sales tax revenue is used to fund public services and programs, including education, healthcare, infrastructure, and social welfare. The revenue generated from sales tax is therefore an important source of income for governments, particularly at the local level.

Sales tax is advantageous for its simplicity and transparency, and for the fact that the tax burden is spread across any given population. However, some argue that sales tax can at times be regressive, meaning that it can have a disproportionate impact on lower-income individuals who spend a larger proportion of their income on goods and services. To combat this, countries have introduced exemptions or reduced rates of sales tax on certain goods and services, while others have introduced value-added tax (VAT), which is a tax collected at every stage of production and distribution. This helps to reduce the impact of sales tax on lower-income individuals by allowing businesses themselves to claim back the tax they pay on their purchases.

The complexity of sales tax regulations can make it challenging for businesses to comply with the laws and regulations. Retailers must keep accurate records of their sales and remit the correct amount of tax to the government. Failure to comply with sales tax regulations can result in penalties and fines. Ultimately, sales tax revenue is used to fund public services and programs, and governments regularly review and update their sales tax laws and regulations to ensure that they are fair, effective, and efficient.

PROPERTY TAX

Property tax is a form of taxation that is imposed on the value of property owned by individuals or businesses. The tax is levied by local governments and is used to fund public services and infrastructure, such as schools, roads, and parks. The amount of property tax owed is calculated based on the value of the property (which is typically assessed by the local government) and the government-set tax rate.

Property tax is an important source of revenue for local governments, providing a steady and reliable source of funding for essential public services. It is also a fair form of taxation, as property owners who benefit the most from public services are required to pay a larger share of the tax burden. One of the benefits of property tax is that it provides a stable source of revenue for local governments, which helps to ensure that essential public services are adequately funded. Property tax revenues are typically used to fund a wide range of services, including public safety, education, transportation, and public health.

It is important to recognize, however, that property tax can be a burden for certain property owners, particularly those who own large or valuable properties. Property taxes are typically assessed based on the value of the property, which means that property owners who own more valuable properties will pay a larger share of the tax burden. This can be challenging for property owners who are on a fixed income or who are struggling financially. Some local governments have introduced measures that alleviate the burden of property tax on lower-income property owners. For example, some governments offer exemptions or reduced rates of property tax for seniors, disabled individuals, and low-income households.

Property tax is, then, an important source of revenue for local governments and is used to fund essential public services and infrastructure. While it can be a burden for some property owners, it is a fair form of taxation that ensures that those who benefit the most from public services pay their fair share. Local governments must ensure that property tax laws and regulations are fair, efficient, and effective, and that they are regularly reviewed and updated to reflect changes in the economy and society.

CORPORATE TAX

Corporate tax is a taxation levied on the profits earned by businesses. It is an important source of revenue for governments and is used to fund a wide range of public services and infrastructure, such as education, healthcare, transportation, and public safety. Corporate tax is imposed on the profits generated by companies once their expenses, such as the cost of goods sold, salaries, rent, and other operational costs, have been deducted. The government determines the tax rate, which usually correlates with the company's income level. In most countries around the world, corporate tax rates vary depending on the size and type of business, as well as the industry in which the business operates.

Corporate tax serves to ensure that businesses contribute to the public welfare and the infrastructure that supports their operations. In order to promote fairness, businesses that earn greater profits are required to pay a higher percentage of their income in taxes. One of the main benefits of corporate tax is that it provides a significant source of revenue for governments, therefore helping to fund essential public services. This revenue is especially important during times of economic downturn, when governments may need to increase spending to support the economy and provide relief to individuals and businesses.

Corporate tax can also encourage businesses to invest in their operations and create new jobs. By reducing their tax burden, companies can reinvest more of their profits into their operations, which can lead to increased productivity and job creation. However, corporate tax can also be a burden for businesses, particularly smaller businesses that may have limited resources. In addition, some businesses may engage in tax avoidance or evasion strategies, such as transferring profits to lower-tax jurisdictions or using other tax loopholes. This can generate a loss of revenue for governments and can be seen as unfair by other businesses and individuals.

In conclusion, corporate tax is an important source of revenue for governments and is used to fund essential public services and infrastructure. While it can be a burden for businesses, particularly smaller businesses, corporate tax is a fair form of taxation that ensures that companies contribute to the public welfare and the infrastructure that supports their operations.

EXCISE TAX

Excise tax, also known as consumption tax, is levied on specific goods or services, typically those that are non-essential or harmful to individuals or society. The tax is usually included in the price of the item or service and is paid by the consumer at the point of sale. Excise taxes are often used to discourage the consumption of 'harmful' goods or services, such as tobacco products, alcohol, and sugary beverages. These taxes are designed to increase the cost of these products and—the intention goes—therefore reduce their overall purchase and consumption.

In addition to promoting public health, excise taxes can also generate significant governmental revenue, which is then used to fund public services such as healthcare, education, and infrastructure. Excise taxes are typically levied at a specific rate per unit of the product in question and are set at a rate determined by the government.

One of the main criticisms of excise taxes is that they can be regressive, meaning that they can have a disproportionate impact on low-income individuals and families. This is because these taxes can represent a larger percentage of their overall income compared to higher-income individuals. To address this issue, some governments have implemented targeted tax credits or other measures to offset the impact of excise taxes on low-income households.

ESTATE TAX

Estate tax, also known as inheritance tax or death tax, is a tax levied on the estate of a deceased person. Typically calculated based on the value of the assets and property owned by the deceased individual at the time of their death, the purpose of estate tax is to generate revenue for the government. The tax revenue generated is then used to fund public services and programs, such as healthcare, education, and infrastructure.

Estate tax is also employed to encourage wealth redistribution and address economic inequality. By imposing taxes on substantial estates, the government can redistribute wealth from the wealthiest individuals to those with fewer resources. However, estate tax has faced criticism for being perceived as unfair and punitive towards the heirs of the deceased. This criticism arises from the notion that heirs may feel burdened by the tax liability, as they may need to sell assets in order to meet the tax obligations, potentially impacting their financial well-being.

However, supporters of estate tax argue that it is a necessary tool for promoting economic equality and preventing the concentration of wealth in the hands of a few individuals. Estate tax laws can be complex and can vary by jurisdiction. Some countries, such as the United States, have federal estate tax laws, while others have estate tax laws that are determined at the state or provincial level.

Overall, estate tax is a controversial topic that can generate strong opinions on both sides. While estate tax can be seen as an effective tool for promoting economic equality and generating revenue for governments, it can also be seen as punitive and unfair to the heirs of the deceased.

HOW TAXES ARE CALCULATED

Marginal tax rates

Marginal tax rates are a tax rate system used to calculate the amount of tax that individuals or businesses owe on their income. Under a marginal tax rate system, the tax rate increases as the taxable income increases, meaning that individuals or businesses will pay different tax rates on different portions of their income, based on their income level.

For example, in a marginal tax rate system, the first portion of an individual's income may be taxed at a lower rate, while the remaining portion is taxed at a higher rate. This is different from a flat tax rate system, where the same tax rate is applied to all income levels.

Marginal tax rates are typically progressive, meaning that higher income earners pay a higher percentage of their income in taxes than lower income earners. This is often done to promote economic equality and to provide government services to those who may need them most.

One of the benefits of a marginal tax rate system is that it can help to promote economic growth and encourage individuals to work and earn more income. This is because individuals will be able to keep a larger percentage of their income as they earn more and will therefore have more incentive to work and earn higher wages. However, marginal tax rates can be complex and difficult to understand, thus making it important that taxpayers to understand how marginal tax rates work and to consult with tax professionals or government agencies to ensure that they are accurately calculating and paying their taxes.

Deductions and exemptions

Deductions and exemptions are two important aspects of the tax system that can help individuals and businesses reduce their taxable income and lower their tax obligations.

Deductions are expenses that can be subtracted from a taxpayer's gross income to reduce their taxable income. Common deductions include expenses related to home ownership, charitable donations, education expenses, and business expenses. Exemptions, meanwhile, are a deduction that is applied to a taxpayer's personal income. Exemptions allow taxpayers to deduct a certain amount of their income from their taxable income, based on the number of dependents they have.

Both deductions and exemptions can help reduce a taxpayer's taxable income, which in turn can lower their tax obligation. However, the amount of the deduction or exemption will depend on the taxpayer's individual circumstances and the specific tax laws in their jurisdiction.

It is important for taxpayers to understand the rules and limitations surrounding deductions and exemptions, as there may be caps or restrictions on certain types of deductions or exemptions. Additionally, taxpayers should keep accurate records of their expenses and deductions to ensure that they are claiming the appropriate deductions and exemptions on their tax returns.

Tax Credits

Tax credits are a tax benefit that can help individuals and businesses reduce their tax liabilities. Unlike deductions, which reduce taxable income, tax credits directly reduce the amount of tax owed. This means that tax credits can reduce tax obligations to a more significant extent than deductions. Tax credits are often designed to encourage certain behaviors or actions deemed in the public interest, such as investing in renewable energy, purchasing an electric vehicle, or adopting a child. Tax credits may also be available for low-income individuals, students, and families with children. Some tax credits are refundable, which means that if the credit exceeds the taxpayer's tax liability, the taxpayer may be eligible to receive a refund for the excess amount. While tax credits are an attractive proposition, taxpayers need to understand tax credits' rules and limitations, as they may be subject to income limits, caps, or other restrictions. Taxpayers should keep accurate records and documentation to support their eligibility for tax credits claimed on their tax returns and should consult with tax professionals or government agencies to ensure that they are accurately claiming any tax credits for which they may be eligible.

Withholding taxes

Withholding taxes are taxes deducted from an employee's paycheck before the employee receives their net pay. Withholding taxes are used to collect income tax, Social Security tax, and Medicare tax from employees on behalf of the government. Employers are responsible for withholding and remitting these taxes to the government on behalf of their employees. The taxes withheld will depend on the employee's income, the number of allowances claimed on their W-4 form, and the tax rates in effect.

Withholding taxes serves several vital purposes. First, they help ensure that employees pay their taxes throughout the year, preventing taxpayers from incurring penalties or interest for underpaying taxes. Withholding taxes also provides a consistent revenue stream for the government, which helps with budgeting and planning.

Employees can adjust their withholding taxes by completing a W-4 form, which allows them to claim more or fewer allowances. However, it is important to understand that if an employee claims too many allowances, they may owe additional taxes at the end of the year. Similarly, if they claim too few allowances, they may receive a large tax refund. In the latter scenario, however, these individuals have also essentially given the government an interest-free loan throughout the year.

LEGAL TECHNIQUES TO LOWER YOUR TAXES

Paying taxes is a necessary obligation that every citizen must fulfill, but it is natural to want to minimize the amount we pay. Fortunately, there are numerous ways to reduce your tax liability legally. You can keep more of your hard-earned money in your pocket by taking advantage of credits, deductions, and intelligent investment strategies.

Before we proceed, please note that some tax-saving strategies only apply to specific groups, such as small business owners or the self-employed. Additionally, the tax code is subject to frequent changes, so it is crucial to stay updated on the latest developments in tax law. You should be able to locate the latest rules relatively easily through an online search.

One common tax-saving strategy is to take advantage of tax credits, which—you will recall—are dollar-for-dollar reductions to your tax bill. Some common tax credits include the Child Tax Credit, the Earned Income Tax Credit, and the American Opportunity Tax Credit for education expenses. Another method is deductions, which reduce your taxable income, which in turn reduces the amount of taxes you owe. Deductions relating to charitable donations, mortgage interest, and state and local taxes are particularly popular. Implementing investment strategies can indeed be effective in reducing one's tax liability. One such strategy involves contributing to tax-deferred retirement accounts, such as a 401(k) or Traditional IRA. By doing so, individuals can lower their taxable income while simultaneously building savings for their retirement. Additionally, investing in municipal bonds can provide tax-free income.

Finally, it is essential to stay informed about changes in tax law and take advantage of new tax-saving opportunities as they arise. For instance, the Tax Cuts and Jobs Act of 2017 introduced several changes to the tax code, including a higher standard deduction and lower tax rates for many taxpayers. In summary, while paying taxes may be unavoidable, there are numerous legal strategies to help reduce your tax liability. You can keep more of your hard-earned money by taking advantage of tax credits, deductions, and investment strategies and staying up to date on the latest tax laws.

Make contributions to a retirement account!

Contributing to a retirement account is one of the best ways to reduce your taxable income. In addition to aiding in retirement savings, utilizing this strategy can also lead to tax savings. This approach is accessible to nearly everyone, regardless of their employment situation. According to Craig Ferrantino, president of Craig James Financial Services in Melville, New York, contributing to a traditional 401(k) or IRA presents an excellent opportunity to lower taxable income. The contributions made to these accounts are deductible from taxable income, resulting in a reduction in the amount of federal tax owed. Additionally, the funds in these accounts can grow tax-free until retirement, providing a powerful incentive for individuals to invest in their retirement accounts.

Another option to consider is Roth accounts, which are funded with after-tax dollars. Although contributions made to Roth accounts do not provide a tax deduction, the funds in the account grow tax-free and can be withdrawn tax-free during retirement. This can be advantageous as it allows individuals to potentially enjoy tax-free income in their retirement years. It is important to note that contributions to workplace 401(k) accounts must be made by the end of the calendar year. In contrast, tax-deductible donations can be made to traditional IRAs until the tax-filing deadline. By contributing to a retirement account, you can secure your future and reduce your tax liability. It is one of life's true win-win situations.

Examine Workplace FSAs for Existence

One way to save on taxes while managing your healthcare expenses is by utilizing flexible spending accounts (FSAs) offered by your employer. With an FSA, you can set aside a portion of your income on a pre-tax basis to fund a report that can be used to pay for various medical expenses, such as insurance copays, deductibles, prescription medications, and even some over-the-counter items. By using pre-tax dollars, you reduce your taxable income. However, note that FSA contributions are subject to certain limits set by the

IRS, and any unused funds at the end of the year may be forfeited, so it is essential to plan carefully.

Many employers also offer FSAs for dependent care expenses, such as childcare or eldercare. Like healthcare FSAs, there are limits to how much you can contribute, and any unused funds may be forfeited at the end of the year. It is essential to review the details of your employer's FSA offerings and determine whether this is a beneficial option based on your anticipated healthcare or dependent care expenses.

Set up a Health Savings Account

If you have an eligible high-deductible medical plan, another effective method to reduce your taxable income and save on taxes is by contributing to a health savings account (HSA). HSAs offer unique tax advantages that benefit individuals and families with qualified medical expenses.

Tatiana Tsoir, a certified public accountant and transformative business and finance coach, underscores the value of HSA contributions due to the tax advantages they offer. Contributions made to an HSA are never taxed when utilized for medical expenses. As a result, HSA donations can be deducted from your taxable income, effectively lowering the amount of taxes you owe. This highlights the significance of HSA contributions as a means to reduce tax liabilities.

Furthermore, the funds in an HSA grow tax-deferred, meaning you are not required to pay taxes on the earnings or interest your account accumulates over time. This allows your HSA balance to grow faster and provides more funds for future medical expenses. Another significant advantage of HSAs is the ability to withdraw funds tax-free for qualified medical expenses. As long as you use the funds for eligible healthcare costs, you will *not* owe any taxes on withdrawals. This can provide significant savings, especially when considering the rising medical care costs.

Unlike flexible spending accounts (FSAs), any balance left in your HSA at the end of the year can roll over indefinitely. This allows you to accumulate funds in your HSA over time, similar to assets in a retirement account. This long-term growth potential makes HSAs attractive for individuals looking to save for future healthcare needs. While this undoubtedly sounds attractive, it remains important to understand the rules and limitations surrounding HSAs, such as contribution limits and qualified medical expenses. Consulting with a financial advisor or tax professional can help you make the most of your HSA and ensure you take full advantage of its tax benefits.

Use Your Side Job to Get Business Tax Deductions

Self-employed individuals, whether full-time entrepreneurs or a part-time freelancer, have access to many tax deductions that can lead to substantial tax savings. Tatiana Tsoir encourages individuals to explore self-employment opportunities, such as side gigs or freelance work, to take advantage of these deductions and maximize their tax savings.

Self-employment opens a range of business deductions that can help reduce your taxable income. For instance, if you use your vehicle for business purposes, you can deduct business-related vehicle mileage. Other deductible expenses include business-related shipping, advertising, website fees, a percentage of your home internet charges used for business, professional publications, membership dues, business-related travel expenses, and office supplies. Additionally, if you pay for your own health, dental, or long-term care insurance, you may be eligible to deduct those premiums.

You can save a significant amount of money by leveraging these deductions effectively. However, navigating the complex rules and regulations established by the IRS is essential and often tricky. Advanced tax savings strategies may require the expertise of an accountant who can help you ensure compliance with tax laws and maximize your tax savings while minimizing the risk of audits or penalties.

Utilize the home office deduction.

If you are self-employed or have a side business, paying especial attention to the potential benefits of claiming the home office deduction is important. This deduction can provide significant tax savings, but it is crucial to understand and adhere to the requirements set by the IRS. To qualify for the home office deduction, you must use a specific area of your home regularly and exclusively for business purposes. This means that the space should be dedicated *solely* to your business activities rather than for personal use. Donald N. Hoffman, partner-in-charge of the Maryland office for Eisner Advisory

Group, emphasizes the importance of adhering to this requirement. To understand how this works, let's introduce a practical example.

For example, suppose that you are a freelance writer and editor. To support your work, you have transformed a spare bedroom into a space that serves *exclusively* as a home office. Imagine that this bedroom accounts for one-fifth of your apartment's total living space. In that case, you can deduct one-fifth (or 20%) of your rent and utility fees as a business expense. This deduction allows you to allocate some of your housing costs toward your business, effectively reducing your taxable income. It is important to consider that if your workspace is located in a shared area, such as the kitchen or living room, it is unlikely to meet the exclusivity requirement for claiming the home office deduction. Therefore, it is unlikely to qualify for the tax benefit associated with the home office deduction. To ensure compliance with IRS regulations and maximize your tax benefits, it is advisable to consult with a tax professional or accountant who can guide you through the process.

Taking advantage of the home office deduction can result in significant tax savings for self-employed individuals and those with a side business. However, you must maintain proper documentation recording your home office expenses and calculating the percentage of your home used for business purposes. By doing so, you can confidently claim the best possible deduction while minimizing the risk of triggering an audit or facing penalties.

Rent Out Your House for Business Meetings

Homeowners can take advantage of the Augusta rule, Augusta exemption, or the 14-day rule to potentially lower their tax liability. These rules permit homeowners to rent out a portion of their home for up to 14 days without having to report the rental income to the IRS. It's crucial to bear in mind that the homeowner's primary residence cannot be used as their primary place of business. For business owners who lack a dedicated home office, this can serve as an opportunity to generate extra income while potentially reducing their tax burden. They can rent a room or area in their home for a business meeting or event and deduct the associated costs from their business taxes. The rental fees do not have to be reported as personal income on their tax return.

Tatiana Tsoir advises caution when taking advantage of this rule. The rental price must be reasonable and align with comparable rental rates for similar spaces in the local market. Maintaining detailed records of the rental arrangement, including the dates of the meeting or event and its purpose, is crucial to substantiate the deduction and ensure compliance with tax regulations. Consulting with a tax professional can provide further guidance on adequately utilizing the Augusta rule and taking advantage of its tax benefits.

CHAPTER FIVE
PURCHASING A HOME

Purchasing a home is a significant milestone in any person's life. However, it is also a major financial decision involving careful planning, thorough research, and attention to detail. Whether you are a first-time homebuyer or are seasoned in the property-buying process, it is of paramount importance that you understand the steps needed to ensure a smooth and successful home purchase. In this detailed chapter, we will delve into various aspects of the home-purchasing process, spanning budgeting, financing, searching for properties, making an offer, inspections, negotiations, and closing the deal.

Assessing Your Finances

Before diving into the home-buying process, it is crucial to evaluate your financial situation. Determine your budget by considering your income, savings, and existing debts. Calculate how much you can comfortably afford to spend on your home and how much you can allocate to a down payment, closing costs, and other expenses associated with homeownership.

- **Establishing Financing Options:** Explore various financing options once you have calculated your budget. You should speak with different lenders and mortgage brokers to understand the types of loans available, such as conventional mortgages, FHA loans, or VA loans. Compare interest rates, loan terms, and eligibility requirements to find the best option for your financial situation.

- **Getting Pre-Approved:** Obtaining a pre-approval letter from a lender is essential as it demonstrates your credibility and helps you understand your price range. To obtain pre-approval, you must provide financial documents such as tax returns, pay stubs, bank statements, and details about your employment history. Pre-approval will give you a clear idea of how much you can borrow and increase your chances of accepting your offer.

- **Engaging a Real Estate Agent:** Working with a qualified real estate agent can simplify home-buying and provide invaluable guidance. Choose an agent who is knowledgeable about the local market, has a good reputation, and understands your specific needs and preferences. They will help you navigate the housing market, locate suitable properties, and negotiate on your behalf.

- **Searching for Properties:** With the assistance of your real estate agent, begin your search for properties that align with your requirements. Consider location, neighborhood amenities, school districts, proximity to work, and transportation options. Use online real estate platforms, attend open houses, and drive through neighborhoods to understand options.

- **Making an Offer:** When you find a property you wish to purchase, your real estate agent will help you prepare and submit an offer to the seller. The request will include the proposed purchase price, contingencies (such as home inspections), desired closing date, and additional terms and conditions. The seller can either accept your offer, reject it, or propose a counteroffer, initiating a negotiation process.

- **Home Inspections:** Once the seller accepts your offer, it is crucial to schedule a home inspection. A professional inspector will assess the property's condition, identifying potential issues or structural problems. The inspection report will objectively evaluate the property's overall condition, helping you make an informed decision about proceeding with the purchase or negotiating repairs with the seller.

- **Negotiating and Finalizing the Deal:** Based on the inspection report, you may negotiate with the seller to address any necessary repairs or adjust the purchase price accordingly. Your real estate agent will be pivotal in these negotiations, advocating for your best interests. Once the negotiations are complete, you must finalize the mortgage application, secure homeowner's insurance, and coordinate with the title company or attorney to prepare for the closing process.

- **Closing the Deal:** The closing process involves signing all the necessary legal documents and transferring property ownership. It typically occurs at a title company, attorneys, or escrow agent's office. You will review and sign the mortgage agreement, settlement statement, and other relevant documents during the closing. You will also pay the closing costs, including loan origination fees, appraisal fees, title insurance, and other administrative expenses.

- **Post-Closing Responsibilities:** After closing the deal and receiving the keys to your new home, several post-closing responsibilities must be considered. Set up utilities, change your address with the post office, and update your information with relevant institutions and service providers. Create a maintenance plan for your home, including regular inspections, repairs, and upgrades. Establishing a budget for ongoing homeownership costs, such as property taxes, insurance, utilities, and maintenance expenses, is also essential.

Home purchasing is a complex process that demands careful consideration, research, and attention to detail. By understanding the steps involved, working with professionals, and making informed decisions, you can confidently navigate the home-buying process. Remember, the information in this chapter is intended to provide a comprehensive overview, but consulting with a real estate professional is crucial to tailoring the process to your specific circumstances.

IMPORTANCE OF HOMEOWNERSHIP

Homeownership holds great significance and provides numerous benefits to individuals, families, and communities. It goes beyond a mere act of acquiring property and encompasses various dimensions that contribute to personal, financial, and communal well-being. Here are some key aspects highlighting the extensive significance of homeownership:

- **Stability and Roots:** Homeownership provides stability, security, and permanence. It offers individuals and families a place to call their own, establishing roots and fostering a sense of belonging. It also provides stability for children, creating a familiar environment and promoting their overall well-being.

- **Financial Investment and Wealth Building:** Homeownership is a long-term financial investment. As property values typically appreciate over time, homeowners can accumulate equity, which can be utilized for various purposes such as future home upgrades, education, or retirement. Moreover, it allows individuals to build wealth and pass it on to future generations, creating a legacy.

- **Pride and Personalization:** Owning a home provides a sense of pride and accomplishment. Homeowners can personalize their living spaces, creating an environment that reflects their unique tastes and preferences. Making changes and improvements to property enables homeowners to create a living area that aligns with their lifestyle and enhances their quality of life.

- **Stability in Housing Costs:** Renting often comes with fluctuating prices, subject to the landlord's discretion. Homeownership provides stability in housing costs since mortgage payments remain relatively stable over the long term, allowing for better financial planning and budgeting.

- **Tax Benefits:** A homeownership offers several tax advantages, such as deducting mortgage interest and property taxes from taxable income, which can result in significant savings.

- **Community and Social Connections:** Homeownership contributes to community development and social connections, with homeowners typically establishing deeper ties within their communities, fostering a sense of camaraderie and social cohesion. b. Homeowners often take pride in maintaining their properties and contributing to the overall aesthetic appeal of the neighborhood, positively impacting property values and community desirability.

- **Sense of Freedom and Autonomy:** Homeownership gives individuals a greater understanding of freedom and autonomy than rental situations. Homeowners have more control over their living environment, allowing for greater Personalization, modifications, and decision-making.

- **Retirement and Long-Term Planning:** Homeownership plays a crucial role in long-term financial planning, especially during retirement. Paying off a mortgage allows individuals to have a debt-free home in their later years, reducing living expenses and providing financial security.

Overall, Homeownership goes beyond mere property ownership. It offers stability, financial benefits, a sense of pride, and a strong foundation for personal and community growth. The importance of Homeownership extends to various aspects of life, making it a worthwhile goal for individuals and families to pursue.

OVERVIEW OF THE HOME PURCHASING PROCESS

The home purchasing process is a complex and multifaceted journey that involves several steps and considerations. It is an exciting yet daunting endeavor, as it often represents one of the most significant financial investments in a person's life. Understanding the overview of the home purchasing process is crucial for a smooth and successful experience.

- **Determine Your Budget:** The first step in buying a home is assessing your financial situation and budget. Consider your income, expenses, and savings to understand how much you can spend on a property. This will help you to establish a realistic price range and avoid overspending.
- **Obtain Pre-Approval:** Getting pre-approved for a mortgage is highly recommended as it demonstrates your financial credibility to sellers and agents. Consult with different lenders to find the best mortgage options, interest rates, and terms that align with your budget and needs.
- **Engage a Real Estate Agent:** Working with a reputable real estate agent can significantly simplify the home-buying process. They

possess a rich knowledge of the local market, access to listings, and negotiation skills. An agent can guide you through property viewings, offer valuable insights, and assist in making informed decisions.

- **Start House Hunting:** Armed with your budget and real estate agent, you are ready to begin the exciting part: the house hunting process. Define your preferences regarding location, property type, size, amenities, and other essential features. Attending open houses, schedule private showings, and explore different neighborhoods to find properties that meet your criteria.

- **Make an Offer:** Once you find a home that meets your requirements, you will need to make an offer to the seller. Your real estate agent will help you prepare the offer letter, considering market conditions, comparable recent sales, and any other necessary contingencies. The seller can accept, reject, or negotiate the offer.

- **Conduct Inspections and Appraisal:** If your offer is accepted, conducting thorough inspections of the property is crucial. Hire a professional home inspector to evaluate the house's condition, identifying any potential issues or repairs needed. Additionally, the lender will require an appraisal to determine the property's market value.

- **Secure Financing:** Finalize your mortgage financing by providing the necessary documents to your lender, including income verification, credit history, and property information. If approved, the lender will evaluate your application, conduct an underwriting process, and issue a loan commitment letter.

- **Closing Process:** The closing process involves several essential steps, including the title search, obtaining title insurance, and signing the final paperwork. A closing agent or attorney will facilitate the transaction, ensuring all legal and financial aspects are appropriately addressed. During the closing, you will pay closing costs that cover fees incurred for the loan, inspections, and other services.

- **Final Walk-Through:** Before closing, you will have the opportunity to conduct a final walk-through of the property. This allows you to ensure that the condition of the property has not declined since your offer was accepted and that any agreed-upon repairs have been completed.

- **Closing and Ownership Transfer:** At the closing stage, you will sign various documents, including the mortgage note and the deed, and will provide the necessary funds for the down payment and closing costs. Once the paperwork is complete and funds are disbursed, the ownership of the property is transferred to you, and you receive the keys to your new home.

- **Post-Closing Considerations:** After the purchase, there are a few post-closing considerations to address. These may include transferring utilities to your name, updating your address with relevant entities, and securing homeowner's insurance. Additionally, it is essential to develop a maintenance plan to preserve the value and condition of your new home.

- **Engage A Real Estate Attorney:** Securing the services of a competent attorney is crucial when overseeing a transaction of this magnitude. This could be one of the most significant purchases an individual will make. Ensuring the protection of your finances becomes imperative. Upon acceptance of their offer, the buyer will be required to provide a down payment during the initial contract signing. It is of utmost importance that the lawyer performs their due diligence to safeguard the entirety of the transaction. Before my career as a real estate agent, I witnessed a buyer who unfortunately lost their down payment during the home-buying process, emphasizing the necessity for extreme caution in such situations.

The home purchasing process is an intricate experience that requires careful attention to detail. While this overview provides a general understanding, consulting with professionals, such as real estate agents, lenders, and attorneys, who can offer personalized guidance and expertise based on your specific circumstances is essential.

ASSESSING YOUR FINANCIAL READINESS

Assessing your financial readiness is essential to achieving your financial goals and securing a stable future. Whether you, the reader, find yourself planning for a significant life event, such as buying a home, starting a business, or simply striving for financial stability, understanding your current financial situation is a critical starting point. But how do you do this accurately? Here are some key areas to consider when assessing your financial readiness:

- **Budgeting and Expenses:** Begin by evaluating your income and expenses. It may sound obvious, but it truly is important to create a comprehensive budget that tracks your monthly income, fixed costs (rent/mortgage, utilities), variable expenses (groceries, entertainment), debt payments, and savings contributions. Analyze your spending habits to identify areas where you can reduce costs and allocate more towards savings or investments.

- **Emergency Fund:** A robust emergency fund is an essential tool when it comes to weathering unforeseen circumstances, such as job loss or costly medical expenses. Assess the adequacy of your emergency fund by considering your monthly payments and setting a target amount to cover at least three to six months' worth. If your fund falls short, prioritize saving and gradually build this up to the necessary level.

- **Debt Management:** Evaluate your debt situation and develop a plan to manage it effectively. List all your debts, including credit cards, student loans, car loans, and mortgages, noting the interest rates, monthly payments, and outstanding balances. Prioritize high-interest debts and consider debt consolidation or refinancing strategies to lower interest rates and accelerate debt repayment.

- **Savings and Investments:** Assess your savings and investment accounts to gauge your progress toward long-term financial goals. Review your retirement accounts, such as 401(k)s or IRAs, and consider increasing contributions if necessary. Explore investment options that align with your risk tolerance and time horizon, such as stocks, bonds, mutual funds, or real estate. Regularly monitor and rebalance your portfolio to ensure it aligns with your objectives.

- **Insurance Coverage:** Adequate coverage is crucial to protecting yourself and your assets from unexpected events. Review your insurance policies, including health, life, home, auto, and disability insurance. Ensure that the coverage amounts are sufficient and evaluate whether adjustments are necessary based on changes in your circumstances or dependents.

- **Retirement Planning:** Assess your retirement savings by estimating and comparing your retirement needs with your current savings. Consider consulting with a qualified financial advisor to evaluate the sufficiency of your retirement accounts, assess investment strategies, and create a personalized plan to meet your retirement goals.

- **Long-Term Financial Goals:** Reflect on your long-term financial goals, such as homeownership, education funding, starting a business, or early retirement. Evaluate your progress towards these goals and—if you are falling short of where you want to be—identify any adjustments to your financial plan that can help you get back on track.

- **Financial Knowledge and Education:** Continually educate yourself about personal finance and investment strategies. Stay updated on financial news, read books, attend seminars, or seek guidance from financial professionals. Enhancing your financial literacy will empower you to make informed decisions and improve your financial readiness.

Regularly reassess your financial readiness as your circumstances change. Life events, such as marriage, having children, or career advancements, may necessitate adjustments to your financial plan. By actively monitoring and addressing your financial readiness, you will be better, more securely equipped to handle unexpected challenges and achieve your long-term financial objectives.

STARTING YOUR HOMEOWNERSHIP GOALS

Starting your homeownership goals is an exciting endeavor that requires careful planning, preparation, and financial readiness. Here are several vital steps to consider when embarking on your homeownership journey:

- **Define Your Homeownership Goals:** Start by clearly defining your homeownership goals. Consider the type of home you desire, such as a single-family house, townhouse, or condominium, and the location that suits your lifestyle and preferences. Determine the number of bedrooms and bathrooms, desired square footage, and any specific features or amenities that are important to you.

- **Assess Your Financial Situation:** Evaluate your financial readiness to determine if you are prepared for the financial responsibilities that come with homeownership. Review your income, expenses, and savings to understand your current financial capacity. Consider stable employment, a good credit score, and a manageable debt-to-income ratio. Assess your ability to make a down payment and comfortably handle mortgage payments, property taxes, insurance, and maintenance costs.

- **Create a Budget and Save for a Down Payment:** Establish a budget that factors in your current expenses and savings goals. Determine how much you can save for a down payment and homeownership costs. Cut unnecessary expenses, reduce debt, and consider additional income streams that can help accelerate your savings.

- **Improve Your Credit Score:** A good credit score is vital when applying for a mortgage. Request a credit report copy and check for errors or discrepancies. Pay off outstanding debts, make timely payments, and avoid taking on new debt. A strong credit history will increase your chances of qualifying for favorable mortgage terms and interest rates.

- **Research Mortgage Options:** Familiarize yourself with the various mortgage options available. Compare offers from different financial institutions to find the most suitable option that aligns with your financial goals and circumstances.

- **Save for Closing Costs and Other Expenses:** Other expenses are associated with purchasing a home beside the down payment. Often the priciest such example is closing costs, which are typically 2% to 5% of the home's purchase price, but other examples are appraisal fees, title insurance, attorney fees, and property inspection fees. Creating a saving plan for these costs and preparing a buffer for unexpected expenses or repairs after moving into your new home.

- **Research and Tour Potential Homes:** Research the real estate market in your desired location. Work with a real estate agent to identify homes that meet your criteria. Attend open houses and schedule viewings to understand the properties better. Take notes, ask questions, and consider the advantages and disadvantages of each property that you view. Remember, patience is often key at this stage of the process.

- **Get Pre-approved for a Mortgage:** Consider getting pre-approved before actively searching for a home. Pre-approval empowers you with a clear understanding of your borrowing capacity and demonstrates your seriousness as a buyer. It can also give you an advantage in competitive housing markets, as sellers often prefer offers from pre-approved buyers.

- **Make an Offer and Complete the Homebuying Process:** Congratulations! If you reach this stage, you must have found your ideal home. Now, you don't want to let it get away. Work together with your real estate agent to make an offer. Negotiate the terms, price, and contingencies with the seller. If your offer is accepted, proceed with a home inspection and appraisal, and work on finalizing the mortgage. Work closely with your lender, attorney, and real estate agent to complete all necessary paperwork and fulfill the requirements for a successful closing.

- **Plan for Homeownership Expenses:** As a homeowner, be prepared for ongoing expenses beyond the initial purchase—budget for property taxes, homeowners' insurance, utilities, maintenance, repairs, and potential renovations. Set aside an emergency fund to handle unexpected home repairs or replacements.

Starting your homeownership goals requires patience, diligence, and careful financial planning. By taking these steps, you can confidently navigate the process and transform your dream of owning a home into a reality. Remember to seek guidance from professionals, such as real estate agents and mortgage lenders, who can provide valuable insights and support throughout the journey.

CHAPTER SIX
CHARITY

Charity is an indispensable element of human society, driven by our desire to alleviate suffering and help those who find themselves in need of basic resources or support. It is a selfless act that embodies compassion, empathy, and the acknowledgment of our shared humanity. Charity can take various—be it the donation of money, goods, time, skills, or expertise—and it can be directed toward an abundance of worthwhile causes, from poverty alleviation and disaster relief to healthcare and social justice.

Voluntarism is a crucial aspect of charity, distinguishing it from other forms of assistance. Indeed, while monetary donations are common and certainly effective forms of help, charity can include volunteering one's time and skills, offering emotional support, or advocating for systemic change. Both nonprofit and for-profit organizations play a vital role in facilitating and coordinating charitable efforts, relying on public support and donations.

Some of the most productive charitable impacts are those which extend beyond immediate assistance and help bridge societal gaps, promote inclusivity, and create a more equitable world. By providing resources and opportunities, charity fosters solidarity and reminds us of our shared responsibility to contribute to the welfare of others. For people's generous offerings to have maximum benefit, however, care must be taken to ensure effective resource utilization, transparency, accountability, and the addressing systemic issues through advocacy and policy changes.

THE PURPOSE OF CHARITY

The purpose of charity is multifaceted, encompassing both the immediate alleviation of suffering and the pursuit of long-term societal change. It is rooted in the recognition of our interconnectedness and the belief in the inherent dignity and worth of every human being. So, let's look at some of the leading purposes underlying charitable actions:

- **Alleviating Suffering:** Above all else, charity serves to alleviate immediate suffering experienced by individuals, families, and communities. Whether it is providing food, shelter, clothing, or medical assistance, charitable acts aim to address the basic, human needs of those in crisis, helping them to regain much-needed stability and hope.
- **Promoting Social Justice:** Charity serves as a catalyst for social change by addressing systemic injustices and promoting equality. It seeks to challenge and dismantle the underlying structures and policies that perpetuate poverty, discrimination, and marginalization.
- **Fostering Empowerment:** Charity endeavors to empower individuals and communities to overcome challenges and improve their circumstances. Beyond immediate aid, charity is committed to offering resources, education, and skills training that enable individuals to become self-sufficient and lead fulfilling lives. Through promotion of education, vocational training, and entrepreneurship, charity breaks the poverty cycle and empowers individuals to create a better future for themselves and their communities.
- **Building Resilience:** Charity plays a crucial role in disaster relief and humanitarian efforts, aiming to build resilience in communities affected by natural disasters, conflicts, or other crises. It provides emergency assistance, facilitates recovery and reconstruction, and supports efforts to enhance preparedness for future challenges.
- **Promoting Social Cohesion:** Charity fosters solidarity and community engagement by uniting people around a common cause. Through volunteerism, philanthropy, and collective action, charity transcends social, cultural, and economic boundaries, and promotes understanding, empathy, and collaboration.
- **Promoting a Culture of Giving:** Charity plays a crucial role in cultivating a culture of giving, in which individuals, communities, and institutions prioritize the welfare of others. By celebrating

philanthropy and highlighting the importance of generosity, charity fosters a sense of collective responsibility and inspires a movement towards creating social change.

In essence, charity goes beyond mere giving. It aims to reduce suffering, advocate for fairness, empower people and communities, foster resilience, enhance social harmony, encourage personal development, and promote a culture of generosity. Charity is a potent catalyst for positive transformation, shaping a kinder, fairer, and more interconnected world.

THE IMPORTANCE OF CHARITABLE GIVING

Charitable giving holds immense importance in our society, serving as a cornerstone of compassion, empathy, and social responsibility. To understand this more completely, we should delve into the multifaceted importance of charitable giving:

- **Alleviating Human Suffering:** Charitable giving is crucial for alleviating the suffering experienced by individuals and communities. It provides vital resources, such as food, clean water, shelter, healthcare, and education, to those in need. This can be a lifeline for individuals facing poverty, illness, natural disasters, or other forms of adversity.

- **Addressing Inequality and Injustice:** Charitable giving plays a pivotal role in addressing systemic inequality and injustice. It recognizes that not everyone starts life on an equal footing and acknowledges the need to level the playing field. By directing resources towards marginalized groups, charitable giving helps bridge socio-economic gaps, promotes equal opportunities, and challenges discriminatory practices.

- **Filling Gaps in Public Services:** Charitable giving compliments and fills gaps in public services, particularly in areas where governmental resources may be limited or insufficient. Nonprofit organizations and charitable initiatives often step in to provide essential services that may not otherwise be available to individuals and communities, including those relating to education, healthcare, disaster relief, environmental conservation, social welfare, and cultural preservation.

- **Nurturing Social Capital:** Philanthropy fosters a sense of social cohesion and strengthens the fabric of communities, encouraging universities to come together, collaborate, and contribute towards a common cause. This sense of social capital promotes a healthier and more interconnected society, where individuals are invested in each other's well-being.

- **Empowering Individuals and Communities:** Charity empowers individuals and communities by providing them with resources, knowledge, and opportunities. It enables access to education, skills training, and economic support, enabling people to break free from the cycle of poverty and lead self-sufficient lives. Charitable giving can also promote entrepreneurship, innovation, and sustainable development, creating pathways for individuals to improve their own circumstances and contribute to the broader economy.

- **Driving Social Innovation:** Charitable giving is a catalyst for social innovation and positive change. By supporting research, development, and pilot projects, it fuels advancements and breakthroughs in areas such as healthcare, education, environmental sustainability, and technology.

- **Cultivating Empathy and Generosity:** Donating to charity is central to cultivating empathy, compassion, and generosity in individuals. By engaging in charitable acts, individuals develop a deeper appreciation for their own blessings and become more inclined to help those less fortunate.

- **Inspiring Collective Action:** Charitable giving serves to inspire collective action and mobilize communities towards a shared purpose. When individuals witness the positive impact of charitable acts, they are more likely to be motivated to join the cause, contribute their resources, or initiate their own philanthropic endeavors. Charitable giving, therefore, has a ripple effect, creating a domino effect of kindness, compassion, and social change.

- **Promoting Personal Fulfillment and Well-being:** Numerous studies have shown that individuals who engage in charitable acts experience increased happiness, a sense of purpose, and improved mental health. Giving therefore not only benefits those in need but also brings joy and fulfillment to the giver.

In summary, charitable giving is a truly powerful force for social change, capable of alleviating suffering, addressing inequality, nurturing social capital, empowering individuals, driving innovation, and inspiring collective action. By engaging in charitable giving, individuals and communities can make a profound and lasting impact on the world, shaping a future that is more compassionate, just, and prosperous for all.

HOW YOU CAN CONTRIBUTE TO CHARITY

Engaging in charitable endeavors is a commendable and rewarding means of creating a positive influence in the lives of others. The possibilities for contributing are vast, and every contribution, regardless of its magnitude, can have an impact. Presented below is an compilation of various ways in which you can contribute to charity. This list is not exhaustive, of course, and an internet search will show you even more methods of helping those in need:

- **Monetary Donations:** One of the most common and straightforward ways to contribute is by making monetary donations. You can donate to well-established charities or organizations that align with your values and causes you care about.
- **Fundraising Events:** Organize or participate in fundraising events such as charity runs, walks, or auctions. This will raise funds and create community spirit.
- **Donate Goods:** Clean out your closet, garage, or attic and donate gently used clothing, furniture, electronics, and household goods to charities or thrift stores. These items can be a great help to those in need.
- **Sponsor a Child:** Consider sponsoring a child in need by providing

financial support for their education, healthcare, and overall well-being.

- **Organize a Charity Drive:** Initiate a local charity drive to collect essential items such as food, clothing, blankets, or school supplies. Distribute these items to local shelters, orphanages, or schools.
- **Support Social Enterprises:** Buy products or services from social enterprises that operate with a mission to address social or environmental issues.
- **Organize a Community Cleanup:** Gather a team of volunteers and organize a community cleanup to remove litter and improve your neighborhood environment.
- **Donate to Disaster Relief:** When natural disasters strike, contribute to relief efforts by donating money, clothing, food, or other essential supplies.
- **Educate Others:** Use social media, write blog posts, or organize informational sessions to share knowledge and encourage others to contribute to causes you care about.
- **Support Fair Trade:** Purchase certified Fair-Trade products, ensuring that producers in developing countries receive fair wages and working conditions.
- **Donate Your Talents:** Share your musical or artistic talents by performing at local charity events or nursing homes.

Remember, the most important aspect of contributing to charity is finding a cause that resonates with you personally. Whether you choose to contribute through donations, volunteering, or raising awareness, your efforts can have a significant impact on the lives of those in need.

THE TRANSFORMATIVE POWER OF GIVING

Let me further explore this subject by referring to a verse from the Bible. Please understand that my intention is not to preach, but rather to illuminate the significance of generosity. In 2 Corinthians 9:6-8, it is stated: "Remember this: Whoever plants sparingly will also harvest sparingly, and whoever plants generously will also harvest generously. Each of you should give what you have decided in your heart to give, not reluctantly or under compulsion, for God loves a joyful giver. And God is able to bless you abundantly, so that in all things at all times, having all that you need, you will excel in every good work."

As we observe billionaires like Bill Gates and Warren Buffett, who initiated the Giving Pledge campaign to encourage affluent individuals to contribute the majority of their wealth to philanthropic causes, it becomes evident that there is immense power in giving. Indeed, it is unlikely that their engagement in philanthropy is solely driven by the desire for tax deductions. As the scripture suggests, when we generously offer our time, money, and knowledge to others, we are rewarded abundantly by God. And for those who are atheist, the message remains: charitable giving rewards us with legacy, fulfillment and reward. The reasons provided by the Charities Aid Foundation, as mentioned earlier, serve as further reinforcement for why individuals should feel compelled to assist their fellow human beings in times of need. We are all interconnected in this world, and events such as the COVID-19 pandemic remind us of our shared humanity.

I have been privileged enough to witness the power of giving firsthand. It was my father who first instilled in me the importance of generosity, but circumstances shifted when he returned to Haiti. At this time, my mother assumed the role of the main provider in our family, wholeheartedly dedicating her time, money, and resources to both acquaintances and strangers alike. As her children, we struggled to comprehend her selfless acts of kindness, which often extended as far as giving away our family's final penny. We often questioned her sanity, especially considering the fact that she had to support seven children as a single mother. Despite the financial hardships we faced when we immigrated to the United States from Haiti, a higher force has always looked after us. In Haiti, we experienced a life of comfort as part of the upper class, thanks to my father's various businesses and properties. We even had domestic staff, such as a maid and a butler. However, we arrived in the United States at the bottom of the socioeconomic ladder. We relied on the kindness of extended family members for shelter and support. I mention this background to emphasize that, regardless of our position on the financial spectrum, my parents consistently prioritized giving to those in need. This exemplifies the nature of charity.

WHY WE GIVE

The act of giving is not solely a transactional process, but rather a transformative one. It has the potential to impact not only the lives of those receiving, but also the lives of the giver themselves. By embracing the power of giving and approaching it with sincerity and compassion, we open ourselves up to a realm of blessings and opportunities that extend far beyond monetary gain. There are several reasons why giving to charity can make us feel good. Let's explore some of these in greater detail.

Giving To Charity Strengthens Personal Values

Giving to charity is a powerful way to strengthen and uphold personal values. When we choose to support causes and organizations that are aligned with our beliefs and principles, it reinforces our commitment to those values and helps shape our identity. By actively giving to charity, we allow ourselves to live in alignment with our beliefs by translating them into tangible actions. This congruence between our values and our behavior fosters a sense of authenticity and integrity, enhancing our overall well-being.

Giving Is More Impactful Than Ever

In today's world, the act of giving holds a greater significance and impact than ever before. One of the foremost reasons for this is the growing interconnectedness of our world. Indeed, emerging technology and social media have bridged geographical gaps, enabling us to connect with causes and communities beyond our immediate surroundings and respond to pressing issues on a global scale. Our ability to give now reaches far and wider, amplifying our impact.

Moreover, our collective awareness and consciousness regarding social and environmental issues has increased. People are becoming more informed and passionate than ever about causes for concern, seeking ways to contribute and make a difference. The increased awareness drives a higher demand for philanthropy and inspires individuals to give back in meaningful ways, creating a ripple effect by encouraging others to join in.

Giving Can Reintroduce Friends and Family to the Importance of Generosity

Giving can serve as a powerful catalyst to reintroduce friends and family to the importance of generosity. In today's fast-paced and often self-focused world, the concept of giving may sometimes take a backseat to personal pursuits and individual aspirations. However, by actively embracing generosity and encouraging others to do the same, we can reignite a sense of empathy, compassion, and community within our social circles.

Leading by example is a powerful way to reintroduce the significance of generosity to those around us. When our loved ones witness our acts of giving and the positive impact it has on both us and others, they are more likely to be inspired and motivated to follow suit. Moreover, initiating conversations about giving can spark thought-provoking discussions and create a safe space for reflection. By sharing personal stories, insights, and our motivation to give, we invite our friends and family to reconsider their own values and priorities and encourage a collective commitment to making a positive difference in the lives of others.

Giving To Charity Builds and Strengthens Community

Giving to charity plays a vital role in building and strengthening communities. When individuals come together to support charitable causes, they create a sense of unity, collaboration, and shared purpose that transcends individual interests and fosters collective well-being. One of the ways giving builds community is by providing crucial support to individuals and groups who are experiencing hardship, poverty, illness, or other forms of adversity within the local area. This not only alleviates immediate suffering but also strengthens the fabric of the community by promoting care, compassion, and solidarity among its members.

Furthermore, charitable giving can empower community members to actively participate in the betterment of their own neighborhoods. By donating time, skills, or resources, individuals can contribute directly to local initiatives and projects that address community-specific issues. This can also foster a ripple effect that extends beyond the immediate beneficiaries. When individuals witness acts of giving within their community, it inspires and encourages others to get involved as well. This creates a culture of generosity and volunteerism, where community members are motivated to contribute their time, talents, and resources to charitable causes.

CHAPTER SEVEN
RENTING vs. BUYING A HOME

Renting versus buying a home is a decision that requires careful consideration based on various factors. Your financial objectives, available resources, and personal preferences all play a role in determining which option is the most suitable for you. Let's delve into the extensive analysis of the advantages and disadvantages associated with both renting and buying a home.

Buying a home has several advantages worth considering. One significant benefit is avoiding the yearly rent increases often imposed by landlords. As a homeowner, you have control over your monthly mortgage payment, providing a level of stability and predictability in your housing costs. Additionally, homeowners can build home equity—which is an asset that grows as the mortgage is paid down and property values appreciate—and enjoy tax benefits such as the ability to deduct mortgage interest, property taxes, and certain repairs made to rental income properties. These deductions can provide significant savings and even lower your overall tax liability.

However, it is important to acknowledge the challenges associated with homeownership as well. Homeowners bear the responsibility of maintaining and repairing their property. Any necessary repairs or renovations must be funded and completed by the homeowner. This can require both financial resources and time. Homeowners are also responsible for covering ongoing expenses such as mortgage payments, property taxes, and homeowners' insurance. These costs should be factored into your overall financial plan.

On the other hand, renting a home offer benefit. Firstly, monthly rent is often lower than a mortgage payment, providing an opportunity for renters to allocate the difference towards investments or other financial goals. Renting also offers flexibility and mobility, as tenants can easily relocate at the end of their lease term or make changes based on personal preferences or job requirements. Furthermore, renters are typically not responsible for property maintenance and repairs, as these obligations fall to the landlord or property management company.

It is worth noting, however, that renting generally does not offer the same level of tax benefits as homeownership. Renters cannot deduct mortgage interest or property taxes since they are not directly responsible for these expenses. This can result in fewer potential tax savings compared to homeowners.

Ultimately, the decision between renting and buying a home is a personal one that should be made based on your specific circumstances and priorities. Carefully consider your financial situation, long-term goals, and lifestyle preferences when making this important choice. If doubt remains, you should seek professional advice from financial advisors or real estate experts who can provide insights and guidance tailored to your unique situation.

THE IMPORTANCE OF CONSIDERING RENTING AND BUYING OPTIONS

The decision between renting and buying a home is a significant one that should not be taken lightly. It is crucial to carefully consider both options and weigh up their respective advantages and disadvantages. Let's explore in extensive detail because it is so crucial to give due consideration to both renting and buying a home.

- **Financial Implications:** The financial aspect is perhaps the most critical factor to consider when deciding whether to rent or buy a home. Renting often requires lower upfront costs, as there is typically no need for a substantial down payment or closing costs. Renters are also not responsible for property taxes, homeowners' insurance, or major repairs, which are typically the burden of the property owner. On the other hand, buying a home—rather than renting—allows you to build equity, benefit from potential property appreciation, and potentially take advantage of tax deductions. However, homeownership also comes with significant financial responsibilities, such as mortgage payments, property taxes, insurance, and maintenance costs. Carefully analyzing your financial situation, future goals, and budget is essential to make an informed decision.

- **Lifestyle and Flexibility:** Another vital aspect to consider is your lifestyle and the level of flexibility you desire. Renting provides more flexibility and mobility, allowing you to relocate when necessary, such as for job opportunities or changes in personal circumstances. Renting is also an excellent option if you prefer not to be tied down to a specific location or if you have an uncertain plan for the future. For this reason, it may be especially popular among younger people. On the other hand, homeownership offers stability and a sense of permanence. If you value establishing roots in a community, personalizing your living space, and having control over property modifications, buying a home may be more suitable for you.

- **Long-Term Goals and Investment Potential:** Consider your long-term goals when making the decision between renting and buying. Buying a home can be seen as an investment, allowing you to build equity over time and potentially benefit from property appreciation. Homeownership also provides a sense of security and can be part of a long-term wealth-building strategy. However, it is critical to remember that the real estate market is not guaranteed, and property values can fluctuate. Renting, on the other hand, may provide more flexibility for investing in other opportunities, such as stocks or businesses. Understanding your long-term financial goals and evaluating the potential return on investment is crucial in making an informed decision.

- **Personal Preferences and Priorities:** Your personal preferences and priorities should also be taken into account. Consider factors such as your desired level of responsibility for property maintenance, the freedom to personalize your living space, and the community or neighborhood you wish to live in. Renting offers less responsibility for property upkeep and the freedom to move easily, while homeownership allows for customization and long-term stability. Additionally, take into consideration your current life stage, future plans, and the potential impact of homeownership or renting on your overall lifestyle and well-being.

- **Market Conditions and Timing:** Lastly, it is essential to consider the current real estate market conditions and timing when making your decision. Real estate markets can vary greatly depending on factors such as location, supply and demand, and economic conditions. Assessing the market conditions can help determine whether it is a favorable time to buy or if it might be more prudent to wait. Additionally, consider factors such as interest rates, housing affordability, and the availability of suitable rental options in your desired area. Again, you may wish to seek professional advice when it comes to interpreting the current market or predicting future changes.

Taken as a whole, the significance of weighing rental and purchasing choices cannot be overstated. This decision encompasses substantial financial consequences, lifestyle factors, future aspirations, individual preferences, and prevailing market conditions. Take the time to thoroughly evaluate each available option, consult with professionals if needed, and make a decision that aligns with your unique circumstances and aspirations. By making the effort to do this now, you will set yourself up for a housing situation that suits your needs, enhances your financial well-being, and brings you closer to achieving your long-term goals.

RENTING A HOME

Renting a home is a significant decision that many individuals and families make at various stages of their lives. Whether you are a young professional, a student, a newly married couple, or someone looking for a change of scenery, renting a home offers a flexible and convenient housing option. In this guide, we will delve into the various aspects of renting a home, covering everything from finding the perfect rental property to understanding the rights and responsibilities of tenants.

- **Determining Your Needs:** Before embarking on the process of renting a home, it is essential to assess your needs and preferences.

Consider factors such as the location, size, and type of property you desire. Think about your budget, desired amenities, and proximity to essential facilities like schools, workplaces, shopping centers, and public transportation. This initial step will help you narrow down your options and focus on properties that meet your requirements.

- **Searching for Rental Properties:** Once you have a clear idea of what you are looking for, it is time to begin your rental property search. There are various resources available to aid this, including online listing platforms, real estate agents, rental magazines, and local newspapers. Online real estate websites and rental applications have become particularly popular in recent years due to their convenience and extensive property databases, particularly in large cities. Utilize these resources to explore different options, view property details, compare prices, and shortlist potential homes.

- **Conducting Property Inspections:** When you come across a property that catches your interest, you should first schedule a property inspection. It is crucial to physically visit the home to assess its condition, layout, and suitability for your needs. During the inspection, pay attention to factors like structural integrity, maintenance, safety features, and any potential issues that may affect your comfort and convenience. Take note of the property's overall cleanliness, functionality of appliances, plumbing, heating, and cooling systems, and the presence of any damage. This information will help you make an informed decision and negotiate terms with the landlord.

- **Understanding Rental Agreements:** Once you have found the perfect rental home, you will need to enter into a rental agreement with the landlord or property management company. A rental agreement is a legally binding contract that outlines the terms and conditions of your tenancy. It covers aspects such as the duration of the lease, rental cost, payment schedule, security deposit, utility responsibilities, pet policies, maintenance procedures, and other relevant rules and regulations. Carefully review the agreement and seek clarification on any clauses or terms that you find unclear or concerning.

- **Financial Considerations:** Renting a home involves financial obligations that extend beyond the monthly rent. Before signing a lease, ensure that you have a clear understanding of the financial responsibility and necessities associated with the rental. Calculate your budget, considering the monthly rent, security deposit, utility bills, renter's insurance, and any additional fees or charges specified in the rental agreement. It is advisable to ensure that you have a financial buffer sufficient to cover unexpected expenses or emergencies that may arise during your tenancy.

- **Tenant's Rights and Responsibilities:** As a tenant, it is essential to be aware of your rights and responsibilities to ensure a harmonious and mutually beneficial landlord-tenant relationship. Familiarize yourself with the local tenancy laws and regulations that govern rental properties in your area. Understand your rights regarding privacy, repairs and maintenance, lease renewal, eviction processes, and the return of the security deposit. Similarly, be mindful of your responsibilities, such as paying rent on time, maintaining the property, adhering to the terms of the rental agreement, and notifying the landlord promptly of any issues or repairs required.

- **Renter's Insurance:** While the landlord is typically responsible for insuring the rental property itself, it is highly recommended that tenants obtain renter's insurance to protect their personal belongings. Renter's insurance provides coverage in the event of theft, fire, natural disasters, or other unforeseen circumstances. It also offers liability protection if someone is injured while visiting your rented home. Evaluate different insurance policies, consider your possessions' value, and choose a policy that offers comprehensive coverage at an affordable price.

- **Moving In and Settling:** Once all the paperwork is complete, and you have signed the lease agreement, the time has come for you to move into your new home. Coordinate with the landlord or property manager to schedule the move-in date and collect the keys. Take this opportunity to document the property's condition through photographs or written descriptions to avoid any disputes when you move out. Ensure that you record any damage that exists at the time of your move-in. Notify utility companies to set up accounts in your name, and update your address with relevant organizations, including banks, government agencies, and service providers. Settle into your new home and familiarize yourself with the local community.

- **Maintenance and Communication:** During your tenancy, promptly report any maintenance or repair issues to the landlord or property management company. Ensure that you follow the designated communication channels specified in the rental agreement. Maintain a record of all communication, including repair requests and the responses you receive from the landlord. Regularly perform basic maintenance tasks, such as cleaning, replacing air filters, and maintaining the property's cleanliness. Taking care of the rental home not only ensures your comfort but also contributes to maintaining a positive relationship with the landlord.

- **Moving Out and Lease Termination:** When the time comes to move out of your rental home, review the terms of your lease agreement regarding notice periods, lease termination, and the return of the security deposit. Provide the required notice to the landlord or property management company in writing, preferably well in advance. Thoroughly clean the property, remove all personal belongings, and restore it to its original condition. Document the property's condition once again to compare it with the move-in documentation. Arrange for a final inspection with the landlord to discuss any concerns and ensure a smooth transition.

THE BENEFITS OF <u>RENTING</u> A HOME

Renting a home offers numerous benefits that make it an attractive housing option for individuals and families. Whether you are a young professional, a student, or someone looking for flexibility and convenience, renting provides several advantages that can enhance your lifestyle and meet your specific needs. Let's explore the extensive benefits of renting a home.

- **Flexibility and Mobility:** One of the primary advantages of renting a home is the flexibility it provides. Renting allows you to have a place to live without the long-term commitment and financial responsibility associated with homeownership. It offers the freedom to relocate easily, whether it's for a job change, personal preference, or any other reason.

- **Lower Initial Costs:** Renting a home typically requires lower upfront costs compared to buying a house. When renting, you are generally responsible for paying a security deposit and possibly the first and last month's rent. These costs are often significantly lower than the down payment and closing costs associated with purchasing a property. Renting allows you to allocate your financial resources elsewhere, such as savings, investments, or pursuing other goals and aspirations.

- **No Maintenance Responsibilities:** One of the significant advantages of renting is that you are not responsible for most maintenance and repair tasks. When renting a home, it is the landlord's responsibility to handle repairs, maintenance, and major replacements, such as fixing plumbing issues, repairing appliances, or addressing structural problems. This relieves you from the financial burden and time-consuming tasks that come with maintaining a property.

- **Access to Amenities and Services:** Many rental properties, especially those in apartment complexes or gated communities, offer a wide range of amenities and services that enhance your living experience. These amenities may include swimming pools, fitness centers, on-site laundry facilities, recreational areas, security systems, and maintenance staff. Renting allows you to access these amenities without the financial and logistical responsibilities of owning and maintaining them yourself.

- **Testing Different Neighborhoods:** Renting a home gives you the opportunity to explore and experience different neighborhoods before committing to a long-term residence. It allows you to get a feel for the community, amenities, schools, and overall ambiance of a particular area. This firsthand experience can help you make an informed decision when you eventually decide to settle down and buy a home.

- **Financial Predictability:** Renting provides financial predictability and stability, allowing you to have a fixed monthly rent payment. This predictability can help you budget effectively and plan your finances with more certainty. Additionally, renting gives you the flexibility to opt for rental properties that fit comfortably within your budget, allowing you to maintain a desirable lifestyle without overextending yourself financially.

- **Reduced Risk of Depreciation:** Real estate markets can be unpredictable, and the value of properties can fluctuate over time. By renting a home, you are not exposed to the risks associated with property depreciation. While homeowners may experience fluctuations in their property's value, as a renter, you can focus on enjoying your living space without worrying about market conditions.

- **Lower Insurance Costs:** When renting a home, you typically only need the renter's insurance, which covers your personal belongings and provides liability protection. This is generally more affordable than homeowner's insurance, which—by contrast—covers the structure of the property as well. This contributes to the overall affordability of renting and allows you to allocate your financial resources to other priorities.

- **Avoiding Real Estate Market Risks:** The real estate market can experience fluctuations and uncertainties that impact property values and the overall housing market. By renting, you are not directly exposed to these risks and can avoid the potential stress and financial implications of a volatile market.

- **Minimal Responsibilities:** Renting a home typically involves fewer responsibilities compared to homeownership. While you have certain obligations as a tenant, such as paying rent on time and abiding by the terms of the lease agreement, the overall responsibilities are generally less demanding and time-consuming. This can be particularly beneficial for individuals with busy lifestyles who prefer, or need, to focus their time and energy on other pursuits, such as work, hobbies, or personal relationships.

SUMMARY

In conclusion, renting a home provides numerous advantages such as flexibility, convenience, and reduced financial commitments compared to homeownership. By carefully considering your needs, conducting thorough research, understanding lease terms, and fulfilling tenant responsibilities, you can have a satisfying renting experience. Effective communication with the landlord, proactive issue reporting, and maintaining a respectful relationship are essential throughout your tenancy. Renting offers benefits like lower initial costs, reduced maintenance responsibilities, access to amenities, financial predictability, and avoidance of certain homeownership risks. It serves as a convenient and customizable housing solution suitable for different lifestyles and life stages, ensuring a comfortable and enjoyable living experience without long-term obligations.

BUYING A HOME

Buying a home refers to the process of acquiring a residential property by entering into a legal agreement with the seller. It involves the transfer of ownership rights and responsibilities from the seller to the buyer. When you buy a home, you become the legal owner of the property, gaining exclusive rights to use and occupy the premises.

The process of buying a home typically involves several key steps, including:

- **Property search:** This involves identifying and exploring available properties that meet your criteria, such as location, size, amenities, and budget. You may utilize real estate agents, online listings, or other resources to find potential homes.
- **Financing:** Unless you are purchasing the property outright with cash, you will likely need to secure financing through a mortgage loan. This involves working with lenders, providing financial documentation, and getting pre-approved for a loan based on your creditworthiness and income.
- **Offer and negotiation:** Once you find a home you wish to

purchase, you make an offer to the seller. Negotiations may take place to determine the final price and terms of the sale, such as contingencies, repairs, or closing costs.

- **Due diligence:** After an offer is accepted, you typically have a *due diligence period* to conduct inspections, appraisals, and gather information about the property's condition, title, and any potential issues that may affect your decision to proceed with the purchase.

- **Closing:** Once all conditions are met, a closing date is set. At the closing, you sign legal documents, pay the remaining funds (including the down payment and closing costs), and complete the transfer of ownership. This is usually done with the assistance of a real estate attorney or title company.

- **Ownership and ongoing responsibilities:** After closing, you officially become the proud owner of your new property. You are responsible for making mortgage payments to your lender, paying property taxes, maintaining homeowner's insurance, and taking care of routine maintenance and repairs.

THE BENEFITS OF <u>BUYING</u> A HOME

Buying a home offers a multitude of benefits that make it a compelling choice for individuals and families. It provides a sense of stability, financial security, control, and numerous long-term advantages. Let's explore the benefits of buying a home in detail.

- **Equity and wealth building:** One of the most significant benefits of buying a home is the opportunity to build equity. As you make mortgage payments, you gradually increase your ownership stake in the property. Over time, as property values appreciate, you can potentially build significant wealth through the equity gained in your home. This equity can then be utilized for future investments, education expenses, or even as a source of retirement income.

- **Stability and permanence:** Buying a home provides stability and a sense of permanence. It offers the assurance of a permanent residence, allowing you to establish roots in a community, build relationships, and create a sense of belonging. This stability is particularly beneficial for families or individuals seeking a place to call home.

- **Control and customization:** Homeownership grants you the freedom to customize and personalize your living space according to your preferences. You have the autonomy to make modifications, renovations, and improvements that suit your lifestyle and reflect your personal taste.

- **Investment and potential appreciation:** Real estate has historically been a solid long-term investment. Buying a home allows you to invest in an asset that has the potential to appreciate over time. As property values increase, you can benefit from the potential growth in your home's value. This appreciation can provide a substantial return on investment and serve as an asset for future financial endeavors.

- **Tax benefits:** Homeownership often comes with various tax benefits. Mortgage interest payments, property taxes, and some closing costs are often tax-deductible, reducing your overall tax liability and increasing your disposable income. These tax advantages can result in significant savings and enhance your overall financial well-being.

- **Stability of housing costs:** Unlike renting, buying a home with a fixed-rate mortgage provides stability in housing costs. With a fixed-rate mortgage, your monthly mortgage payments remain consistent throughout the loan term. This stability allows for better budgeting and financial planning, providing peace of mind and reducing financial uncertainty.

- **Pride of ownership:** Owning a home often brings a sense of pride and accomplishment. It represents a significant achievement and a symbol of success. Homeownership is an accomplishment that many aspire to, and it can contribute to overall happiness and fulfillment.

- **Retirement planning:** Buying a home is often seen as a crucial component of retirement planning. As you pay off your mortgage, you eliminate a significant monthly expense, providing financial relief during retirement. Additionally, owning a home can serve as a valuable asset to tap into for funding retirement or as a source of rental income if you choose to downsize or relocate.

- **Privacy and security:** Homeownership offers greater privacy and security compared to rental properties. You have control over who enters your home and can implement security measures to protect your property and loved ones.

- **Freedom to make long-term decisions:** When you own a home, you have the freedom to make long-term decisions without the restrictions of a lease agreement. You can renovate, expand, or modify your property to accommodate changing needs or lifestyle choices, creating a living space that evolves with you and meets your specific requirements.

SUMMARY

In conclusion, buying a home entails a significant financial commitment but offers a range of advantages. It provides stability, a sense of ownership, and the opportunity to build equity while creating a personalized living space. Homeownership brings benefits such as equity and wealth building, control and customization, investment potential, tax advantages, stable housing costs, pride of ownership, retirement planning, privacy, security, and the freedom to make long-term decisions. These advantages make buying a home an appealing choice for individuals seeking financial security, stability, and the ability to establish a place they can truly call their own.

CHAPTER EIGHT

BUDGETS

WHAT IS A BUDGET?

In my quest for the perfect definition of 'budget', I stumbled upon a concise explanation which goes as follows:

"A budget is a comprehensive plan, typically financial, for a defined period, often spanning a month or a year. It encompasses various aspects such as projected sales volumes, revenues, resource allocation (including time, costs, and expenses), environmental considerations like greenhouse gas emissions, other impacts, assets, liabilities, and cash flows. Budgets serve as strategic roadmaps, enabling companies, governments, families, and other organizations to express their planned activities in quantifiable terms."

As evident from the above definition, a budget is employed by households, businesses, and governments to outline their income and expenditure for a specific duration. This duration could range from monthly to quarterly or even yearly. In a household context, individuals can list their monthly bills and expenses while considering their income to assess if it will sufficiently cover their financial obligations. Alongside a budget statement, employing additional financial resources is essential for tracking expenses and gaining insights into expenditure patterns. Understanding where one's money goes is the initial step towards resolving financial challenges.

Businesses rely on cash flow statements to gain a comprehensive overview of their financial activities, identifying revenue-generating products/services and areas for cost reduction. Individuals and families should adopt similar tools for informed financial decision-making.

Taking inspiration from how businesses manage finances, individuals can establish a separate fund, similar to petty cash, for unforeseen or minor purchases. Petty cash refers to a small amount of money kept on hand to facilitate small expenses. Setting aside funds specifically for minor purchases, easily accessible and potentially in an interest-bearing account, becomes crucial.

The financial decisions of the US government reflect citizens' attitudes and behaviors. Concerns arise from the continuous printing of money without tangible asset backing, leading to currency stability and value concerns. Reliance on external borrowing strains the economy and questions financial independence. Insufficient income tax revenue collection forces the government into difficult choices regarding resource allocation, potentially leading to spending on non-essential items.

Nation-building efforts incur significant costs for taxpayers, echoing the struggles of households living paycheck to paycheck. Both the government and many American households tend to spend money as if it were endless, leading to substantial debt and financial hardships in the long run. Borrowing money from credit card companies at high interest rates exacerbates the issue. The practice of budgeting connects these issues and offers a solution. Many American families overlook or fail to effectively implement budgeting. Without budgeting, money disappears quickly, perpetuating financial instability.

In summary, businesses benefit from cash flow statements, and individuals/families should adopt similar tools. Establishing separate funds for minor purchases, inspired by petty cash, proves beneficial. Concerns arise from the US government's deficit, currency stability, external borrowing, insufficient tax revenue, and nation-building costs. The tendency to overspend and accumulate debt is shared by the government and households. Budgeting addresses these issues, but many families fail to implement it effectively, leading to financial instability. We will now explore some key financial rules one at a time, delving deep into how each of them can aid your financial life.

KEEP TRACK OF YOUR EXPENSES

In today's fast-paced and consumer-driven world, it is all too easy to lose sight of our spending habits and find ourselves in a financial predicament. The seemingly harmless daily purchases, occasional splurges, and overlooked expenses can quickly add up, leaving us wondering where all our hard-earned money went. This is where keeping track of your expenses comes into play. By diligently monitoring and recording your expenditures, you can gain invaluable insights into your financial habits and make informed decisions that pave the way to long-term financial success.

The first step in keeping track of your expenses is to create a comprehensive system that works for you. This might vary from person to person. Some of you may favor a traditional pen-and-paper style, while others may prefer utilizing one of the many mobile phone budgeting applications that have emerged in recent years. Whichever route you choose, the goal is to make the process as seamless and effortless as possible, ensuring that you consistently record your expenses without feeling overwhelmed or burdened by the task. Tracking your expenses should be a rewarding task, not a chore!

Once you have established your tracking system, the next step is to diligently record every single expense. Remember, this does not only include major purchases; it must factor in every small transaction that you make. Yes, that includes the morning coffee run, the cake you grabbed at the store, and that pesky mobile phone bill. Don't forget to go through your monthly subscriptions, too – you might even discover one or two that you had forgotten about entirely! Every dollar spent adds up over time, and by capturing even the smallest expenses, you gain a comprehensive understanding of your spending patterns and identify areas where you can potentially cut back or adjust.

One effective approach to tracking your expenses is to categorize them. By assigning each expense to specific categories such as housing, transportation, groceries, entertainment, and so on, you can gain deeper insights into how you allocate your funds. Your mobile banking app might be able to help you out with this, since many banks now offer this feature as part of their application. It can be worthwhile to go through your recent transactions and categorize each of them – you might just be surprised which comes out on top. From a practical perspective, this categorization enables you to identify trends, pinpoint areas of overspending, and allocate your resources more effectively.

Regularly reviewing and analyzing your expense records is crucial for making informed financial decisions. Take the time to evaluate your spending patterns on a weekly, monthly, and yearly basis. Look for any unexpected or recurring expenses that stand out. Are there specific categories where you consistently exceed your budget? By asking yourself these questions and studying your expense data, you can identify potential financial pitfalls, prioritize your spending, and make necessary adjustments to stay on track with your financial goals.

Keeping track of your expenses not only provides financial insights but also instills a sense of accountability and mindfulness in your spending habits. When you actively engage in recording and reviewing your expenditures, you become more conscious of your financial choices. Next time you are about to make an impulse purchase, perhaps you will be discouraged after seeing your recent expense breakdown. This increased awareness empowers you to make deliberate decisions about your spending, distinguishing between wants and needs, and ultimately, contributing to a more disciplined and intentional financial lifestyle. In the long run, every small difference can add up.

In addition to tracking expenses, setting realistic financial goals is crucial. Whether it's saving for a house, paying off debt, or planning for retirement, clear objectives guide spending decisions and emphasize the importance of accurate expense records. By aligning expenses with goals, progress can be made towards achieving them, leading to financial stability and security.

Remember, tracking expenses is an ongoing commitment. It requires discipline, consistency, and a willingness to confront financial habits. However, the rewards are worth the effort. By actively monitoring and categorizing expenses, regularly reviewing records, and aligning spending with goals, control over finances is gained, smarter choices are made, and a brighter financial future is created. Start today and embark on the journey to financial success by tracking expenses.

GIVE YOURSELF A LIMIT ON UNBUDGETED SPENDING (PETTY CASH)

Petty cash refers to small, unplanned expenses that may arise unexpectedly or fall outside the scope of a predetermined budget. By self-imposing a limit on what you are willing to fork out for such expenses, individuals can exercise control over their discretionary spending and ensure that it does not spiral out of control.

The first step in implementing this strategy is to determine an appropriate limit for your petty cash. It is hard for me to advise on any limit for you, since the situation will vary considerably from person to person. Therefore, your limit should consider your financial situation, income, and overall budget. Remember not to be too strict with yourself. Instead, aim to strike a neat balance between responsible financial management and enough flexibility to account for some unforeseen expenditure.

Now that your limit is in place, it is essential to set clear guidelines and rules regarding the use of petty cash. Communicate these guidelines to yourself or your team, ensuring that everyone understands the purpose of the limit and how it should be utilized. Emphasize the importance of adhering to the limit and encourage accountability in managing petty cash expenses.

The inherent problem with petty cash spending is that it can be tricky to keep track of – after all, these are so-called insignificant purchases. To aid the tracking process, then, it is advisable to maintain a separate record dedicated exclusively to these expenses. Whenever a petty cash expense arises, make a detailed note of its monetary value, date, and purpose. In the long run, these records will serve as a transparent and tangible means of monitoring your petty cash expenditures, allowing you to identify any patterns, trends, or areas where adjustments may be necessary. When you go back to review your expenses later, you will thank yourself for writing this information down!

It is important to note that setting a limit on unbudgeted spending does not mean eliminating all spontaneous or unplanned expenses. Instead, it serves as a tool for maintaining financial discipline and ensuring that discretionary spending remains within manageable boundaries. By implementing a limit on unbudgeted spending, individuals and organizations can exercise greater control over their finances and foster a culture of responsible spending. This practice helps prevent overspending, reduces the risk of accumulating unnecessary debt, and promotes financial mindfulness. Ultimately, it contributes to a healthier financial outlook, enabling individuals and organizations to allocate resources more effectively and work towards their broader financial goals.

SAVE FOR LARGE EXPENSE PURCHASES

Saving for large expense purchases is a proactive approach that allows individuals to save for items or experiences that require a substantial financial commitment. Such instances may include buying a new car, purchasing a new home, booking your dream vacation, or funding your child's tuition fees. No matter what the nature of the expense is, the steps you should follow remain the same. Firstly, of course, you should identify the specific goal or item you are saving for. Then, carefully determine the approximate cost of the purchase and establish a realistic timeframe for achieving it. This will help you set a savings target and create a savings plan that aligns with your financial capabilities.

With the goal and savings plan established, you are ready to begin your mission! First and foremost, it is essential that you allocate a portion of your regular income specifically for the purpose of achieving your goal. Without this, it will take far longer to reach your ambitions! This allocation is best done by creating a separate savings account or designating a regular, specific portion of your existing savings towards the large expense goal. By treating these savings as a priority, you ensure that it receives reliable contributions and remains untouched until the desired amount is accumulated. You should be prepared that this may sometimes require you to make certain lifestyle adjustments or sacrifice immediate gratification for the long-term benefit of achieving your desired purchase. It will be worth it in the end though!

Automating your savings is a helpful strategy to support this. Using your mobile or online banking services, you should be able to set up an automatic transfer from your regular income account to your designated savings account on a regular basis. This way, the savings process becomes effortless and consistent, ensuring that progress is made towards your large expense purchase without requiring continuous manual effort. For this to be effective, however, you must maintain good discipline and resist the temptation to dip into this ever-growing savings account. This level of discipline and focus will enable you to accumulate the necessary funds within the desired timeframe.

It is important to remain flexible throughout the saving process, as is true in all financial endeavors. Put some time aside to periodically reassess your savings plan and make adjustments as necessary. If you find that your initial savings rate is not sufficient or if circumstances change, such as an increase in income or a decrease in the cost of the desired purchase, consider revising your savings plan accordingly.

Lastly, celebrate milestones along the way to stay motivated. Recognize and reward yourself for achieving savings milestones or reaching a certain percentage of your target. This positive reinforcement helps maintain momentum and encourages continued commitment to your savings goal.

Saving for large expense purchases requires patience, discipline, and careful planning. By setting clear goals, establishing a savings plan, maintaining consistency, and staying focused, you can successfully accumulate the necessary funds and ultimately make your desired purchase without incurring excessive debt or financial strain. This approach empowers you to take control of your finances, prioritize your spending, and work towards achieving your long-term financial aspirations.

CUT DOWN YOUR MONTHLY BILLS

Reducing monthly bills is a proactive approach to managing expenses and optimizing financial resources. By identifying areas for cost reduction and implementing strategies to minimize recurring bills, you can free up funds for savings, debt repayment, or other financial goals. This practice involves evaluating, negotiating, and potentially adjusting your lifestyle and service providers.

Start by assessing your current monthly bills and pinpointing areas where costs can be cut. Common areas to consider include utilities (electricity, water, gas), cable or satellite TV, internet services, mobile phone plans, insurance premiums, subscriptions, and other recurring expenses.

Begin with utility bills. Seek opportunities to conserve energy and water, such as using energy-efficient appliances, adjusting thermostat settings, and being mindful of water usage. Explore switching to lower-cost providers or alternative energy sources if available in your area. Review your cable or satellite TV packages and eliminate unnecessary services or add-ons to reduce expenses. Consider more affordable options like streaming services for entertainment needs.

Next, review your internet and mobile phone plans. Research alternative providers and compare pricing to ensure you are getting the best value for your needs. There are various websites that can help you to do this! Be prepared to compare rates with other providers and leverage that information in negotiations. Loyalty does not always result in the best deal, so be open to switching providers if necessary.

Insurance premiums are another area where you can potentially save money. Shop around for competitive rates and consider adjusting your coverage based on your current needs. However, it is important to remain cautious when making changes to ensure you maintain adequate coverage for your specific situation. Take a critical look at your subscriptions, such as streaming services, gym memberships, magazine subscriptions, and other recurring expenses. Determine which ones are truly essential and bring you value and consider canceling or downgrading those that are not providing significant benefits.

Cutting down your monthly bills requires proactive engagement and ongoing evaluation. Regularly review your bills, assess your options, and remain vigilant for opportunities to reduce costs. By making conscious choices, negotiating with service providers, and being mindful of your spending habits, you can successfully reduce your monthly expenses, increase your financial flexibility, and work towards achieving your financial goals.

EAT AT HOME MORE

Eat at home more" is a suggestion or advice that emphasizes the benefits of preparing and consuming meals at home rather than dining out or ordering takeout. This practice encourages individuals and families to prioritize home-cooked meals as a way to improve their overall well-being, save money, and foster healthier eating habits.

By choosing to eat at home more frequently, individuals have greater control over the ingredients and the cooking methods used in their meals. This allows for healthier food choices, as home-cooked meals typically include more nutritious ingredients such as fruits, vegetables, lean proteins, and whole grains.

Outside of your bodily health, eating at home can boost your financial health too. Dining out or ordering takeout regularly can be expensive, as the cost of restaurant meals often includes additional charges for service, overhead, and convenience. By preparing meals at home, individuals can significantly reduce their expenses and allocate those savings towards other financial goals or necessities. Compare the cost of a meal at your favorite restaurant with the cost of you cooking a similar dish in your own kitchen... the savings can be astonishing!

Moreover, eating meals at home encourages family bonding and social inter-action. When everyone gathers around the table for a home-cooked meal, it creates an environment for quality time and strengthens relationships. Family members can engage in meaningful conversations, share stories, and connect on a deeper level. By disconnecting from technology and other distractions, the focus is shifted to enjoying each other's company and fostering a sense of togetherness.

To incorporate more home-cooked meals into your routine, it is helpful to plan your meals in advance. This can involve creating a weekly meal plan, making a grocery list, and ensuring you have the necessary ingredients on hand. Meal prepping and batch cooking can also save time and make it easier to prepare meals during busy weekdays. Additionally, try to explore new recipes, cooking techniques, and flavors. This can make the experience of cooking at home more enjoyable and exciting, in turn motivating you to do it more often.

While it may not be feasible to eat at home for every meal, making a conscious effort to increase the frequency of home-cooked meals can have a positive impact on your health, finances, and overall lifestyle. It encourages mindful eating, allows for greater dietary control, and facilitates a stronger connection with loved ones. By embracing the practice of eating at home, individuals and families can experience a range of benefits and establish a foundation for healthier, more fulfilling lifestyles.

DISPOSAL INCOME

Disposable income refers to the amount of money that individuals or households have available for spending or saving after deducting taxes and essential expenses from their total income. It represents the portion of income that is not allocated to fixed obligations such as taxes, rent or mortgage payments, insurance premiums, and other necessary expenses. Higher disposable income generally provides individuals with greater financial freedom, allowing them to enjoy a higher standard of living, save for the future, and make discretionary purchases or investments.

Disposable income is a key indicator of an individual's or household's financial flexibility and ability to meet discretionary spending needs and savings goals. It provides a clearer picture of the funds available for non-essential purchases, leisure activities, investments, and building wealth.

To calculate disposable income, start with the total income earned from various sources, including wages, salaries, bonuses, investments, and any additional income. From this total, taxes such as income tax, Social Security contributions, and Medicare taxes are deducted. The resulting amount is the disposable income.

Disposable income plays a significant role in the economy as well. When individuals have more disposable income, they are likely to increase their spending, which stimulates consumer demand and drives economic growth. On the other hand, a decrease in disposable income can lead to reduced consumer spending, impacting businesses and overall economic activity.

It is important to note that while disposable income represents the funds available after essential expenses and taxes, individuals and households should exercise responsible financial management. This includes budgeting, saving, and making informed spending decisions to ensure long-term financial stability and meet financial goals.

PAY DOWN YOUR DEBT

Paying down your debt involves making regular payments towards outstanding loans, credit card balances, or other forms of debt with the aim of decreasing the overall debt burden. When individuals borrow money, they are obligated to repay the principal amount along with any interest or fees accrued over time. Failing to manage debt effectively can lead to financial stress, high interest costs, and limited financial freedom.

Paying down debt offers several benefits. First and foremost, it helps individuals regain control of their finances by reducing the burden of monthly debt payments. By making consistent and timely payments, individuals can gradually decrease their outstanding balances and work towards becoming debt-free. This can alleviate financial stress and provide a sense of accomplishment. Moreover, debt often comes with interest charges, which can significantly increase the total amount repaid over time. By making extra payments towards the principal balance, individuals can reduce the overall interest paid and potentially shorten the repayment period.

Responsible debt management, including making regular payments and reducing outstanding balances, can also positively impact one's credit score. A higher credit score opens doors to better interest rates, loan options, and increased financial opportunities in the future. With that said, let's look at a few options for how to pay down your debt:

- **Create a budget:** Assess your income and expenses to determine how much you can allocate towards debt repayment each month. Prioritize debt payments and adjust your spending habits accordingly.
- **Pay more than the minimum:** Whenever possible, pay more than the minimum required payment on your debts. This helps to reduce the principal balance faster and minimize interest charges.
- **Consider debt consolidation:** If you have multiple debts with varying interest rates, consolidating them into a single loan or credit card with a lower interest rate can simplify repayment and potentially save money.
- **Snowball or avalanche method:** Two popular debt repayment strategies are the snowball method and the avalanche method. The snowball method involves paying off the smallest debt first and then using the freed-up funds to tackle the next smallest debt. The avalanche method prioritizes paying off debts with the highest interest rates first, saving more on interest costs in the long run.
- **Seek professional advice if needed:** If you are struggling to manage your debt or facing financial hardship, consider seeking guidance from a financial advisor or credit counseling service. They can provide personalized advice and assist in developing a debt repayment plan.

Paying down debt requires discipline, perseverance, and a commitment to financial well-being. By gradually reducing debt balances, individuals can improve their financial situation, achieve greater financial freedom, and work towards their long-term financial goals.

STOP USING YOUR CREDIT CARD ON A NORMAL PURCHASE

Using credit cards as a payment method for everyday items like groceries, dining out, clothing, or entertainment can be tempting. In some instances, however, it is not advisable. There are arguments on both sides here: While credit cards undoubtedly offer convenience and flexibility, relying on them for routine expenses can have certain drawbacks.

The primary concern is the potential accumulation of credit card debt. When individuals use their credit cards for everyday purchases without promptly paying off the balance, it can lead to carrying a revolving debt with accumulating interest charges. Paying with cash or a debit card, by contrast, ensures that individuals only spend what they have available, promoting responsible financial habits and preventing the accumulation of credit card debt. Furthermore, when relying on credit cards, it is easy to lose track of spending and overspend without realizing the impact until the monthly statement arrives. By using cash or a debit card, individuals can maintain a more tangible understanding of their available funds and can make more conscious spending decisions.

Nevertheless, it is important to note that credit cards can offer certain benefits when used responsibly. They provide an opportunity to build a positive credit history and earn rewards or cashback (a percentage of the total cost refunded to your card) on eligible purchases. Additionally, credit cards can offer additional consumer protections and security features compared to cash or debit cards.

To use your credit card responsibly, commit to reviewing your credit card statements and assessing your current credit card usage patterns. Identify areas where you tend to rely on credit cards for normal purchases and consider alternative payment methods. If you have existing credit card debt, focus on paying it off as quickly as possible. Make more than the minimum payment each month to reduce the principal balance and minimize interest charges.

CHAPTER NINE
SET SPECIFIC GOALS

Setting specific goals is essential for personal growth and success. Back in my dating days, I would frequently ask potential partners about their aspirations. Questions like "Do you have a five-year goal?" or "Where do you see yourself in three years?", I figured out, were excellent tools for identifying individuals who shared my drive for personal and professional enrichment.

Goals represent the endpoint of our desires and aspirations. By setting specific goals, we avoid leaving things to chance. Life is too precious to rely solely on luck or happenstance. Let's draw an analogy with the game of football to illustrate this point. The purpose of the game is to reach the opposing team's end zone, but there are formidable linebackers weighing over 300 pounds attempting to impede progress. However, with every touchdown scored, we moved closer to the field goal. Life operates on a similar principle. When we strive to achieve something, we may encounter adversity, but by perseverance and overcoming obstacles, we progress toward our desired outcomes.

Just as a football team follows the plan, preparation, and motivation set by their coach, we must also have a plan and prepare for success in life. In fact, proper preparation and planning are crucial for achieving our goals. I once heard an inspirational speaker say that every athlete has a coach, every successful actor has an acting coach, every bodybuilder has a physical trainer, and every accomplished business owner has a mentor. This raises an important question: as an ordinary individual, what guidance do you have? In high school, we had guidance counselors, but beyond that, we often found ourselves surrounded by the noise of family, friends, and coworkers.

While this book can act as one of your mentors, I strongly urge you to explore other literary works as well. In the recommended reading section at the end of this book, I have compiled a list of titles that are closely aligned with the subject matter and have personally left a profound impact on me. I truly implore you to explore their wonderful pages and continue to enrich your knowledge of this topic.

THE IMPORTANCE AND BENEFITS OF SETTING SPECIFIC GOALS

Setting specific goals is of utmost importance in personal and professional development. Goals provide a sense of direction, purpose, and focus in our lives. They serve as guiding principles that help us prioritize our actions, make informed decisions, and channel our efforts towards meaningful achievements. To fully appreciate the importance of setting specific goals, we ought to consider the benefits that can be yielded from doing so. Of these, there are plenty.

One of the primary advantages of setting specific goals is that they provide clarity. When we have a clear vision of what we want to accomplish, we are better equipped to create a roadmap to reach our desired destination. Without specific goals, we may find ourselves wandering aimlessly, unsure of what we truly want or how to get there. By clearly defining what we want to achieve, we eliminate distractions and concentrate our energy on tasks and actions that align with our objectives. This heightened focus allows us to make efficient use of our time and resources, enabling us to work towards our goals with purpose and intention.

Moreover, specific goals enable us to measure our progress. When we have clear parameters and benchmarks to assess our advancement, we can track our journey and celebrate milestones along the way. This sense of progress not only boosts our motivation but also provides a sense of fulfillment and satisfaction as we witness ourselves moving closer to our goals. In other words, having specific goals enables us to break complex objectives down into smaller, actionable steps, making them more manageable and achievable. This systematic approach promotes efficiency, allowing us to make steady progress and optimize our productivity.

Setting specific goals also helps us overcome obstacles and challenges. When faced with adversity, having a clear goal in mind allows us to stay focused and resilient. It provides us with a sense of purpose and determination, enabling us to find creative solutions and persevere through difficult times. Without a specific goal, we may easily get discouraged or lose sight of the bigger picture when faced with obstacles. Moreover, as we make progress towards our goals, achieving milestones and overcoming obstacles, we develop a sense of accomplishment and belief in our abilities. This newfound confidence not only propels us forward but also radiates in other areas of our lives. It positively impacts our relationships, career prospects, and overall well-being, as we embrace a can-do attitude and approach challenges with optimism.

Furthermore, specific goals enhance our decision-making process. When we have a clear objective, it becomes easier to evaluate different options and choose the path that aligns with our goals. Specific goals act as filters, helping us prioritize our time, energy, and resources towards actions that contribute to our desired outcomes. This focused decision-making process prevents us from getting distracted or wasting our efforts on activities that do not contribute to our long-term aspirations.

In addition, setting specific goals promotes personal growth and development. Goals challenge us to step out of our comfort zones, acquire new skills, and broaden our horizons. They push us to continuously learn, adapt, and improve ourselves. The process of striving towards specific goals allows us to discover our strengths, overcome limitations, and unlock our full potential. Through this growth process, we gain valuable insights, learn from setbacks, and develop resilience. Each step towards our specific goals becomes an opportunity for self-discovery and self-improvement, allowing us to unlock our full potential and become the best versions of ourselves.

Lastly, setting specific goals provides a sense of accountability. When we articulate our goals to ourselves and others, we create a sense of responsibility and commitment. Although it can often seem scary, sharing our goals with trusted individuals, such as friends, family, or mentors, can provide support, encouragement, and valuable feedback. This external accountability helps us stay on track, stay motivated, and increase our chances of success. Like all forms of self-assessment, this ultimately enables us to identify areas for improvement, celebrate our successes, and remain committed to achieving our specific goals.

In summary, setting specific goals is a fundamental aspect of personal and professional development, and one that comes with an abundance of benefits. Goals provide direction, clarity, measurement, resilience, enhanced decision-making, personal growth, and accountability. By setting specific goals, we empower ourselves to lead purposeful lives, maximize our potential, and turn our aspirations into tangible achievements. So, let us take the time to reflect, define, and set specific goals that will guide us towards a future filled with fulfillment, success, and personal satisfaction.

Avoiding leaving things to chance or luck

Leaving things to chance or luck is a risky proposition that can often lead to disappointment, missed opportunities, and a lack of progress. Instead, taking control of our lives and actively shaping our future through deliberate actions is a far more effective and rewarding approach.

One of the key reasons to avoid relying on chance or luck is the uncertainty it brings. Leaving things to chance means relinquishing control and placing our fate in the hands of external factors that are beyond our influence. This lack of control can breed anxiety, as we become passive observers of our lives, hoping for favorable outcomes without actively working towards them. In contrast, taking charge and setting clear intentions empowers us to navigate the uncertainties of life with greater confidence and resilience.

Leaving things to chance also overlooks the importance of personal responsibility. By taking proactive steps and setting specific goals, we acknowledge that we are the architects of our own lives. We understand that our choices, actions, and efforts play a crucial role in shaping our future, and this allows us to embrace our power to create positive change and achieve meaningful results. This in turn promotes a proactive mindset. Instead of waiting for opportunities to come our way, we actively seek them out. We identify our passions, interests, and goals, and then take deliberate actions to pursue them. This proactive approach shifts our mindset from passivity to proactivity, allowing us to remain attuned to new possibilities, be open to growth, and establish ourselves as proactive creators of our own destiny.

Moreover, avoiding leaving things to chance instills a sense of purpose, direction and personal growth in our lives. When we set specific goals, we have a clear vision of what we want to achieve and why it matters to us. This sense of purpose helps us make decisions that align with our values and aspirations, ensuring that we stay on track and make progress towards our desired outcomes. By actively seeking opportunities for growth, learning, and self-improvement in this way, we become lifelong learners, constantly expanding our knowledge, skills, and perspectives. This commitment to personal growth enhances our capabilities, boosts our confidence, and equips us to overcome challenges with resilience and adaptability.

Fostering a sense of direction and purpose

Fostering a sense of direction and purpose is a transformative and enriching experience that can profoundly impact our lives. When we have a clear sense of where we are headed and understand the why behind our actions, we become more focused, motivated, and fulfilled. It is through fostering a sense of direction and purpose that we can navigate the complexities of life, overcome challenges, and ultimately create a meaningful and rewarding existence.

Fostering a sense of direction and purpose brings a multitude of benefits to our lives. Firstly, it brings clarity and focus. When we know where we are headed and understand our purpose, we can filter out distractions and prioritize what truly matters. We become more efficient and effective in pursuing our goals, as we are guided by a clear vision and sense of purpose. This clarity allows us to make decisions with greater confidence and reduces the sense of being overwhelmed by life's multitude of options and possibilities.

A sense of direction and purpose also ignites motivation and drive. When we have a compelling reason behind our actions, we are more likely to stay committed and dedicated to our goals. This in turn helps us persevere during challenging times, as we are connected to something deeper than immediate gratification or external validation. With a sense of direction and purpose, we tap into an intrinsic source of motivation that sustains us on our journey. As a result, our actions become meaningful and purposeful, contributing to our personal growth and the betterment of the world around us. We feel a sense of accomplishment as we make progress towards our aspirations and witness the positive impact of our efforts.

Finally, holding a sense of direction and purpose also provides resilience and resilience during challenging times. When faced with obstacles or setbacks, having a clear direction and purpose can help us maintain perspective and stay committed to our goals. This resilience allows us to navigate through difficult circumstances with strength and determination, emerging stronger on the other side.

Motivating and driving personal growth and development

Personal growth and development are motivated and driven by a lifelong quest of self-actualization, self-improvement, and self-discovery. It is the proactive and deliberate pursuit of ongoing education, development, and expansion in many facets of our lives.

Setting specific goals is a key driver of this pursuit. We give ourselves a sense of direction and purpose by establishing precise and definite goals, which can direct us toward our intended outcomes by acting as milestones and markers along the way. They assist us in narrowing our focus, setting priorities for our work, and tracking our advancement. Setting both short- and long-term objectives enables us to develop a roadmap for our own personal improvement.

The knowledge that we can influence our own lives is at the core of what motivates and propels personal growth and development. We are aware that we actively contribute to our own development rather than simply watching it happen. This mentality change is essential because it encourages us to accept accountability for our choices, actions, and results. It forces us to go past our apparent boundaries, accept difficulties, and venture outside of our comfort zones.

Continuous learning is vital for personal growth and development. It expands our horizons, skills, and knowledge. It involves seeking new experiences, acquiring fresh information, and mastering new abilities. Engaging in activities like reading, attending workshops, having meaningful conversations, or pursuing education all contribute to our learning journey. By embracing a growth mindset and committing to lifelong learning, we open more opportunities for personal advancement.

Self-reflection and self-awareness play crucial roles in personal growth and development. Understanding ourselves, including our strengths, weaknesses, values, and beliefs, allows us to make conscious choices and align our actions with our true selves. Through self-reflection, we identify areas for improvement, challenge limiting beliefs, and create plans for personal growth. It also cultivates qualities like self-compassion, resilience, and adaptability, which help us navigate obstacles and setbacks inherent in the growth process.

Promoting personal development has a transformative impact not only on our own lives but also on society. As we mature and develop, we enhance our ability to serve communities and positively influence the world. Our personal growth can inspire and energize others, setting off a chain reaction of progress and positive change. By relentlessly pursuing growth and development, we contribute to individual and societal transformation.

THE ANALOGY OF GOALS IN LIFE TO A FOOTBALL GAME

Drawing an analogy between goals in life and a football game provides a compelling framework for understanding the importance of setting goals, working towards them, and overcoming obstacles along the way. Just like in a football game, where the ultimate objective is to score touchdowns and win the game, in life, we strive to achieve our goals and find fulfillment and success.

It might sound like a strange comparison initially but stay with me while we break this down together. In a football game, players and teams have a clear goal in mind: to move the ball across the field, overcome opposition, and score points. Similarly, in life, setting goals gives us a sense of direction and purpose. Yet this purpose will seldom be realized easily. Just as football players face challenges in the form of opposing players who try to stop the progression of the player with the ball, we will all encounter obstacles and difficulties in our pursuit of goals. However, like determined football players, we must persevere, adapt our strategies, and keep pushing forward.

The comparison can go beyond these superficial aspects, too. For instance, consider how football is a game that requires teamwork, coordination, and effective communication among players to achieve success. In football, each player has a specific role and contributes their unique skills and abilities to move the team forward. In life, likewise, collaboration and support from others play a significant role in our personal growth and goal attainment. Surrounding ourselves with a supportive network of family, friends, mentors, and colleagues can provide guidance, encouragement, and valuable insights to help us navigate challenges and achieve our goals.

Preparation is vital in football, and this translates to life as well. Before a game, football teams spend hours practicing, strategizing, and analyzing their opponents. Similarly, in life, preparing for our goals involves acquiring knowledge, honing our skills, and developing a plan of action. Remember the topic of this chapter... setting specific goals! By doing so—in football and life alike—we increase our chances of success and are better equipped to face any challenges that come our way.

Life—like football games—follows a timeline with defined quarters. By setting both short-term and long-term goals, we can break down our aspirations into achievable steps and milestones. This approach enables us to track our progress, make necessary adjustments, and celebrate our accomplishments along the way. Just as a football game brings out the best in players, pursuing our life goals unlocks our full potential. It drives us to develop new skills, expand our knowledge, and cultivate qualities like perseverance, determination, and resilience. Moreover, it imparts valuable lessons on teamwork, leadership, and the significance of strategy and planning.

Finally, and most enjoyably of all, the objective of reaching the opposing team's end zone in football leads to immense fulfillment. Just as football players experience a sense of accomplishment and joy when they score a touchdown, reaching our own personal end zones in life brings a deep sense of fulfillment and satisfaction. It validates our hard work, dedication, and perseverance, and provides a tangible representation of our progress and growth.

See, this analogy doesn't sound so far-fetched anymore, does it? Ultimately, this analogy of goals in life to a football game reminds us that success is not solely defined by the outcome but by the effort, growth, and lessons learned throughout the journey. It emphasizes the importance of setting specific goals, embracing challenges, working as a team, and staying focused on the end objective. Finally, the analogy of goals in life to a football game serves as a powerful metaphor for understanding the significance of setting goals, facing challenges, and persisting in the pursuit of our aspirations. By applying the principles of focus, preparation, teamwork, and discipline, we can navigate the field of life, score our own personal touchdowns, and achieve the fulfillment and success we desire.

Overcoming obstacles and adversity

Overcoming obstacles and adversity is an inevitable part of life's journey. It is in the face of challenges that our true strength and resilience are tested, and it is through overcoming these obstacles that we grow and develop as individuals. Whether they are physical, emotional, or mental hurdles, the process of overcoming adversity is a transformative experience that shapes our character and propels us towards personal growth.

Obstacles come in various forms and sizes. They can be external, such as financial difficulties, health issues, or unexpected setbacks, or internal (such as self-doubt, fear, or limiting beliefs). Regardless of their nature, obstacles have the potential to disrupt our plans, dampen our spirits, and derail our progress. However, it is our response to these challenges that determines our ability to overcome them and move forward.

One of the key elements in overcoming obstacles is developing a resilient mindset. Resilience is the ability to bounce back from setbacks, adapt to change, and maintain a positive outlook in the face of adversity. It involves cultivating mental strength, emotional intelligence, and a growth mindset. By reframing obstacles as opportunities for growth and learning, we can approach them with a sense of determination and optimism.

In the process of overcoming obstacles, we often discover hidden strengths and capabilities within ourselves. Adversity pushes us outside our comfort zones and forces us to tap into our inner resources. We may uncover untapped talents, problem-solving skills, and the ability to think creatively. Through persistence and perseverance, we develop a sense of self-efficacy and gain confidence in our ability to overcome future challenges.

Overcoming obstacles also requires developing effective strategies and seeking support when needed. It is important to analyze the situation, identify possible solutions, and take decisive action. This may involve seeking guidance from mentors, seeking advice from experts, or leaning on the support of friends and family. Collaboration and teamwork can provide fresh perspectives, alternative solutions, and emotional support during difficult times.

It is worth noting that overcoming obstacles is not a linear process. It involves setbacks, failures, and moments of doubt. However, these moments of adversity can be valuable teachers. They provide opportunities for self-reflection, self-discovery, and personal growth. By learning from our mistakes, adapting our strategies, and staying committed to our goals, we become more resilient and better equipped to navigate future challenges.

Finally, overcoming obstacles cultivates qualities such as perseverance, discipline, and determination. It teaches us the value of hard work, patience, and persistence. It strengthens our character, builds our confidence, and fuels our motivation to keep moving forward. Through the challenges we face, we gain a deeper understanding of ourselves, our priorities, and what truly matters to us. By embracing obstacles as opportunities for growth, we can navigate life's ups and downs with grace, determination, and an unwavering spirit.

Progressing closer to achieving desired outcomes

Progressing closer to achieving desired outcomes is a driving force that fuels personal growth and fulfillment. When we set specific goals and work diligently towards them, we create a roadmap for success and embark on a journey of continuous improvement. The process of progressing towards our desired outcomes is marked by milestones, achievements, and a sense of purpose that propels us forward.

One of the most rewarding aspects of progressing towards our desired outcomes is the sense of accomplishment that comes with each step. As we make progress, we experience a sense of fulfillment and satisfaction, knowing that we are moving closer to realizing our aspirations. This sense of achievement boosts our self-confidence, enhances our self-belief, and inspires us to strive for even greater heights.

Progress also provides a tangible measurement of the effectiveness of our strategies. It allows us to assess our performance, adjust, and refine our approach. By tracking our progress in this manner, we can identify areas of improvement, build on our strengths, and address any obstacles that may hinder our advancement. This iterative process of growth enables us to optimize our actions and increase our chances of success.

Furthermore, progressing towards desired outcomes cultivates a growth mindset—a mindset that embraces challenges, values effort, and sees setbacks as opportunities for learning and improvement. With a growth mindset, we view progress as a continuous journey rather than a destination. We understand that setbacks and obstacles are natural parts of the process, and we are committed to overcoming them and learning from them. This mindset empowers us to persist in the face of adversity, embrace feedback, and adapt our strategies as we strive for our goals.

Progressing towards desired outcomes also promotes self-motivation and a sense of purpose. As we witness our progress, we become more motivated to continue working towards our goals. The incremental steps we take reaffirm our commitment and dedication, igniting a sense of passion and enthusiasm for the journey ahead. We become driven by a sense of purpose, knowing that our efforts are bringing us closer to achieving the outcomes we desire.

Moreover, the process of progressing towards desired outcomes opens doors to new opportunities and possibilities. As we make progress, we expand our knowledge, skills, and networks, which in turn create new avenues for growth and advancement. Each step forward opens up a world of possibilities, enabling us to explore new territories, take on new challenges, and uncover hidden potential within ourselves.

Progress is not limited to the achievement of specific outcomes; it encompasses personal development and self-discovery. Along the journey, we gain valuable insights, learn from our experiences, and develop new perspectives. We become more self-aware, understanding our strengths, weaknesses, and areas for improvement. This self-awareness allows us to make informed decisions, align our actions with our values, and create a life that is meaningful and fulfilling.

Finally, progressing closer to achieving desired outcomes is a transformative process that drives personal growth and development. It fuels our sense of accomplishment, cultivates a growth mindset, and empowers us to overcome challenges. With each step forward, we gain confidence, refine our strategies, and expand our opportunities. Progress not only leads us towards our desired outcomes but also shapes us into the best version of ourselves. It is through the journey of progression that we discover our true potential and create a life of purpose and fulfillment.

SEEKING GUIDANCE AND MENTORSHIP

Seeking guidance and mentorship is a powerful catalyst for personal growth and development. It is a proactive step towards realizing our full potential and achieving our goals, allowing us to obtain valuable insights and perspectives from individuals who have walked the path before us. Mentors, whether they are experienced professionals, seasoned experts, or wise advisors, can provide us with a roadmap toward our goals, opening our eyes to potential pitfalls and offering strategies for success, and sharing invaluable knowledge that can accelerate our progress.

By seeking guidance and mentorship, we gain access to a vast network of resources and opportunities. Mentors often have extensive networks that they can tap into, connecting us with like-minded individuals, industry professionals, and potential collaborators. These connections can open doors, expose us to new ideas and perspectives, and provide us with valuable support and opportunities for growth.

Seeking guidance and mentorship also provides a sense of accountability. When we have a mentor or guide, we have someone who holds us accountable for our actions and progress. They provide encouragement, support, and gentle nudges that can keep us on track towards our goals. This accountability ensures that we stay focused, committed, and motivated, even during challenging times.

Furthermore, guidance and mentorship are essential for personal growth. They create a safe and supportive environment where we can reflect, discover ourselves, and improve. Mentors offer advice, encourage critical thinking, and empower us to make our own decisions. In turn, this provides us with a much-needed appreciation for one crucial fact: we do not have to go through life alone. Learning from others ought not to be seen as a sign of weakness, but as a tool for accelerating our progress. It shows our commitment to growth, willingness to learn, and desire to reach our potential.

In summary, guidance and mentorship are catalysts for personal growth. They provide valuable insights, resources, and opportunities. They offer support, accountability, and inspiration. Embracing mentorship opens doors to possibilities, accelerates our progress, and unlocks our true potential. It is through the guidance and mentorship of others that we navigate life's complexities, conquer challenges, and become the best versions of ourselves.

Recognizing the importance of mentors in various fields

Recognizing the importance of mentors in various fields is crucial for personal and professional growth. Mentors play a pivotal role in guiding individuals on their journey towards success, offering invaluable insights, advice, and support based on their own experiences and expertise. Let's look at some of these below:

- **ACADEMIA**: In the world of academia, mentors are vital for aspiring scholars and researchers. They provide guidance in choosing research topics, designing experiments, analyzing data, and publishing findings. Mentors in academia help navigate the complexities of the academic landscape, offering advice on securing funding, establishing collaborations, and advancing one's career. They also serve as role models, inspiring students and early-career researchers to pursue excellence and make significant contributions to their respective fields.

- **BUSINESS**: In the business world, mentors can be instrumental in shaping the careers of aspiring entrepreneurs and professionals. They share their business acumen, providing guidance on strategy, operations, marketing, and financial management. Mentors offer insights on building effective networks, developing leadership skills, and making sound decisions. Their mentorship can accelerate career advancement, foster innovation, and instill the necessary skills and mindset for success in the competitive business landscape.

- **THE ARTS**: In creative fields such as art, music, and writing, mentors provide invaluable guidance and inspiration. They offer constructive feedback, helping aspiring artists refine their craft and find their unique voice. Mentors share their expertise on technique, style, and artistic expression, nurturing the creative talents of their mentees. Through their guidance, mentors help individuals navigate the challenges of the creative process, overcome self-doubt, and develop a strong artistic identity.

- **SPORTS**: In the realm of sports, mentors are instrumental in shaping the careers of athletes. They provide technical expertise, helping athletes improve their skills, refine their techniques, and reach peak performance. Mentors also offer guidance on physical conditioning, mental toughness, and sportsmanship. They inspire athletes to set ambitious goals, overcome setbacks, and pursue excellence in their chosen sport.

It is vital to note that the importance of mentors extends beyond the individual level. Mentors contribute to the overall growth and development of their respective fields by nurturing the next generation of professionals. By passing on their knowledge and expertise, mentors ensure the continuity and advancement of their fields. They contribute to the collective knowledge and skills of the industry, fostering innovation, and driving progress.

Overall, recognizing the importance of mentors in various fields is essential for personal and professional growth. Mentors provide guidance, support, and inspiration, helping individuals navigate the complexities of their chosen paths. By fostering a mentorship culture, we can nurture talent, drive innovation, and ensure the continued growth and success of various fields.

Acknowledging the limitations of relying solely on family and friends

While family and friends play a significant role in our lives, it is important to acknowledge the limitations of relying solely on them for guidance and support. While their love and support are invaluable, family and friends are often biased by their personal relationships with us. They may have preconceived notions about our capabilities, preferences, and limitations and—as such—their advice (while certainly pure in intention) may be influenced by their emotional connection to us. Thus, relying solely on their input may limit our ability to explore different possibilities and challenge ourselves to reach new heights.

Moreover, family and friends may not possess the necessary expertise or experience in specific areas of interest and may lack the breadth of experience that we require. While their support is invaluable in providing emotional encouragement, and should not be overlooked entirely, seeking guidance from individuals who have achieved success or possess deep knowledge in relevant fields can offer specialized insights and practical strategies. As we outlined above, mentors, coaches, or industry experts can provide guidance based on their extensive experience and help us navigate complex challenges.

Furthermore, relying solely on family and friends for support can put a strain on relationships. While they may be willing to help, constantly leaning on them for guidance and support can create a dynamic of dependency. This can lead to feelings of burden, strain relationships, and hinder our ability to develop self-reliance and problem-solving skills. Even more concerning, there is a risk of us becoming complacent and comfortable within our existing support network. Seeking guidance from mentors, coaches, or other professionals challenges us to take ownership of our growth and actively seek out opportunities for improvement. It empowers us to set higher standards for ourselves and pursue personal development with intentionality.

In conclusion, while family and friends provide essential emotional support, it is crucial to recognize the limitations of relying solely on them for guidance and support. Seeking guidance from a diverse network of mentors, experts, and professionals allows us to access specialized knowledge, gain different perspectives, and foster personal growth.

CONTINUOUS LEARNING AND PERSONAL GROWTH

. In today's dynamic and competitive environment, the importance of continuous learning cannot be overstated. The world is constantly evolving, with new technologies, ideas, and opportunities emerging at a rapid pace. Thus, to stay relevant and thrive in such an environment, we must commit ourselves to lifelong learning. This involves actively seeking out new information, exploring different perspectives, and acquiring new skills that align with our personal and professional goals. Now more than ever, this can yield a plethora of attractive benefits.

- **Adaptability and Resilience:** By embracing a growth mindset and remaining open to new experiences, we cultivate the ability to navigate challenges and embrace change. As we expand our knowledge and skills, we become more flexible in our thinking, more capable of finding innovative solutions, and more confident in tackling unfamiliar situations. Continuous learning equips us with the tools to embrace ambiguity, overcome obstacles, and thrive in the face of adversity.

- **Personal Growth:** As we engage in the process of learning, we not only acquire new knowledge and skills but also gain a deeper understanding of ourselves. We uncover our strengths, weaknesses, passions, and values, which enables us to make more informed choices and pursue paths that align with our authentic selves.

Continuous learning helps us develop self-awareness, self-confidence, and a sense of purpose, all of which contribute to personal growth and fulfillment.

- **Intellectual Stimulation:** Continuous learning also fosters a sense of curiosity and intellectual stimulation. It allows us to explore new topics, engage in critical thinking, and broaden our perspectives. By expanding our knowledge base and exposing ourselves to diverse ideas, cultures, and disciplines, we cultivate a richer understanding of the world and develop a more nuanced worldview. This not only enhances our personal growth but also enables us to connect with others and contribute to the betterment of society.
- **Adaptability:** In today's knowledge-based economy, skills become obsolete at an accelerated rate. To remain competitive and seize new opportunities, we must embrace a mindset of continuous upskilling and reskilling. By consistently upgrading our skills and knowledge, we enhance our professional marketability and increase our chances of success in a rapidly evolving job market.

In summary, continuous learning and personal growth are essential for navigating an ever-changing world and realizing our full potential. By committing ourselves to lifelong learning, we equip ourselves with the knowledge, skills, and mindset necessary to adapt, innovate, and thrive. Continuous learning not only expands our horizons and enhances our professional prospects but also fosters personal development, self-awareness, and a deeper understanding of the world around us. Embracing a mindset of continuous learning is a powerful tool for personal growth, fulfillment, and success.

The misconception that learning ends after formal education.

One of the most widespread fallacies is the idea that our educational journey ends the day we collect our degree or graduate from college. Nothing could be further from the truth than this. Learning is a continuous process that transcends the boundaries of formal schooling and lasts a lifetime.

While formal education does give students a solid foundation in information and skills, it is only the first step on our educational journey. In the quick-paced, always-evolving world of today, new knowledge, technology, and ideas are continually emerging. We run the risk of becoming outdated in our knowledge and abilities if we restrict our learning to what we learned in school.

After completing formal education, learning continues to have many advantages. It enables us to maintain our intellectual curiosity, widen our horizons, and maintain our relevance in both our personal and professional lives. Learning increases our curiosity, keeps our wits sharp, and quenches our hunger for information. It gives us the chance to learn about new topics, form new interests, and unearth abilities or passions.

Additionally, studying outside of the classroom broadens our perspective on the world and fosters critical thinking. It aids in the refutation of presumptions, the examination of conventional wisdom, and the growth of a broader outlook. We can manage complicated situations, make knowledgeable judgments, and meaningfully participate in discussions and debates by actively seeking fresh information and opposing opinions.

Continuous learning fosters both professional and personal development. It gives us fresh knowledge and abilities that might lead to interesting chances and professional success. We can learn specialized skills, keep up with market trends, and adjust to new technology and techniques through seminars, online courses, books, or mentorship. We put ourselves in a position for personal fulfillment, career success, and the capacity to grab new opportunities by embracing lifelong learning.

Additionally, learning outside of the classroom encourages growth and improvement in oneself. It enables us to discover new hobbies, artistic outlets, and ways to improve our general wellbeing. We can pick up useful life skills that make our daily lives more enjoyable and fulfilling, like cooking, gardening, or playing an instrument. Continuous learning also encourages us to venture outside of our comfort zones, take on new challenges, and develop our resilience and adaptability.

It is vital to understand that learning outside of the classroom doesn't always include going to graduate school or investing a lot of time and money in structured programs. Numerous easily accessible and reasonably priced options are available, including websites, libraries, community classes, and mentorship programs. The secret is to adopt a growth mentality, keep a hunger for information, and actively look for chances to learn and develop. A lifelong learning mentality enables us to live full lives, make significant contributions, and constantly work to improve ourselves.

Emphasizing the lifelong process of self-improvement

Self-improvement, like learning, is a lifelong adventure that is crucial to our personal development and general wellbeing. Positive change, learning new abilities, forming healthy routines, and cultivating a growth mindset are ongoing processes. To reach our maximum potential, live satisfying lives, and have a positive influence on both us and people around us, we must place a strong emphasis on the lifelong process of self-improvement.

The understanding that there is always space for progress is one of the fundamental components of self-improvement. We all have the capacity to change for the better, regardless of our age, upbringing, or current circumstances. This can involve enhancing our physical, mental, emotional, and spiritual wellbeing, among other aspects of our existence. Knowing who we are and understanding our values, beliefs, and aspirations is essential to figuring out where we may develop and get better. We learn about our ideas, feelings, and behaviors through self-reflection, introspection, and self-assessment. This self-awareness forms the basis for making deliberate decisions that are in line with our beliefs and intended outcomes.

Alongside the obvious component of learning new concepts and abilities, self-improvement also includes developing one's emotional quotient, resiliency, and self-care skills. It includes increasing emotional intelligence, efficient stress and emotion management, and the development of constructive coping mechanisms. We may improve our relationships, our ability to make decisions, and live more balanced and satisfying lives by taking care of our emotional wellbeing. Furthermore, adopting healthy habits and activities that promote our wellbeing and personal growth is another aspect of self-improvement. This could entail engaging in regular physical activity, eating healthfully, prioritizing self-care activities, developing mindfulness and appreciation, and creating healthy connections.

Self-improvement is not a solitary endeavor. On our path to self-improvement, seeking support from mentors, coaches, therapists, or joining groups of like-minded people can offer direction, accountability, and encouragement. Our growth and personal development can be substantially enhanced by having meaningful conversations, exchanging experiences, and learning from other people's viewpoints. By making self-improvement a lifelong commitment, supported by those around us, we may continue to grow, thrive, and build meaningful, fulfilling lives.

Encouraging reading and seeking knowledge from diverse sources

Accepting a wide variety of sources and actively seeking knowledge through reading is a potent stimulant for one's intellectual progress, personal development, and ability to comprehend the world more fully. Books, articles, research papers, and other literary works are all examples of informational resources that provide us with a plethora of knowledge, viewpoints, and facts that can greatly improve our lives.

Reading is more than just a leisure activity; it opens doors to new perspectives, encounters, and knowledge. When we read books, we go on a journey of discovery, learning about various cultures, historical moments, technological advancements, philosophical ideas, and much more. Reading stimulates our creativity, piques our curiosity, and creates countless opportunities.

We expose ourselves to a variety of ideas and opinions by seeking information from a variety of sources. This diversity tests our assumptions, broadens our comprehension, and encourages critical thought. By engaging with a variety of viewpoints, we can get a nuanced and comprehensive understanding of complicated subjects, empowering us to make wise decisions, actively participate in discussions and debates, and develop into well-informed world citizens. It is essential to have a comprehensive awareness of many cultures, societal challenges, and global trends in an age of rapid information sharing and interconnectedness.

Additionally, reading improves our language, empathy, and communication abilities. As we read and hear writing from other authors, we pick up new words, expressions, and idioms that improve our own language skills. This language development helps us communicate better verbally and in writing, but it also helps us express ourselves more effectively. Moreover, we can put ourselves in the shoes of characters in literature who come from a variety of backgrounds, ethnicities, and experiences. Through their experiences, we learn more about the human condition, grow empathetic toward all viewpoints, and acquire a greater understanding of the complexity of the world we live in.

It's significant to remember that pursuing information goes beyond reading books. It entails actively seeking information from a range of sources, including scholarly journals, reliable websites, documentaries, podcasts, and meaningful interactions with subject-matter experts. We can continuously change, adapt, and stay relevant in a world that is constantly changing if we embrace a lifetime dedication to learning and intellectual curiosity. With that said, let's immerse ourselves in the written word, investigate novel concepts, and embrace knowledge's transformational potential.

CIRCLE OF FRIENDS

The famous quote, "Show me your friends, and I'll show you your future," attributed initially to Dan Pena, carries a profound truth. However, my mother also imparted a similar wisdom to me. She used to say, "If you keep hanging out with the wrong crowd from the neighborhood, you're bound to find yourself in trouble with the law."

This powerful statement emphasizes the significant influence that our social circle has on our lives. The people we surround ourselves with are pivotal in shaping our identity and determining our path. Spending considerable time with a particular group of individuals inevitably leads to the adoption of their thoughts, beliefs, and values, and our behaviors and mannerisms gradually tend to mirror those of our companions.

Given these profound effects, we must carefully select the individuals we associate with. Surrounding ourselves with positive, supportive people who genuinely want us to succeed is essential. When our friends positively influence us, motivating and inspiring us to become better versions of ourselves, keeping them in our inner circle is beneficial. However, it is essential to remember that we must also take charge of our own lives and be leaders in our own right. We cannot let anyone steer us towards negative paths or derail our progress. Our responsibility is to make conscious decisions that align with our values and aspirations, irrespective of external influences.

Additionally, having a supportive network of individuals who celebrate our achievements and share in our aspirations is invaluable. These people genuinely care about our well-being and happiness and provide the encouragement and assistance we need to reach our goals. However, we must recognize that not everyone may share our dreams or be genuinely happy about our success. Some individuals may even feel threatened or resentful when we thrive in life (think back to the *Keeping up with the Joneses* section earlier in this book).

By actively choosing positive influences, being leaders in our lives, and surrounding ourselves with supportive individuals who genuinely want us to succeed, we can create a future filled with growth, happiness, and accomplishment. It is crucial to be discerning about the company we keep and to foster relationships that foster our personal and professional development.

CHAPTER TEN
GIFTED MIND

I love reading. It is a joy that I have embraced throughout my life. It is no surprise, then, that people often ask me a certain question: *What book has impacted you most profoundly?* My answer, every time, is "Gifted Hands" by Ben Carson. I first read this book in my twenties, at which point its powerful message forever shifted my perspective on life. When I think back now, "Gifted Hands" taught me the invaluable lesson that with determination, focus, and hard work, I could accomplish anything I set my mind to. Inspired by this revelation, I wanted to aptly name this chapter "Gifted Mind," as our minds serve as the driving force behind our achievements and aspirations.

Within each of us lies a unique set of skills and abilities bestowed upon us by our Creator. It is our responsibility to discover these gifts and nurture them to make a positive impact on society. Much like the story of Ben Carson in "Gifted Hands," who relentlessly pursued excellence despite the challenges he faced, I could relate to his journey. I, too, grew up in humble beginnings.

When I was just ten years old, my family and I immigrated to the United States from Haiti due to the political instability that arose from the overthrow of the president. It was during my elementary school years that an unexpected opportunity presented itself. Our class had the chance to order books through a subscription service. I can still recall how I returned home that day with a spring in my step, eventually mustering up the courage to ask my mother for some money. Little did I know that those books would become a turning point in my life. Perhaps my mother knew this on my behalf, though, for she handed over the money and fully embraced my eagerness to read. For that, I am eternally grateful.

The arrival of those books transformed my life in ways I could have never imagined. Despite the impoverished circumstances in which I lived, reading those books transported me to a different mental and intellectual environment. They opened my eyes to new possibilities and broadened my horizons. Through the pages of those books, I discovered worlds beyond my own, met remarkable characters, and absorbed valuable knowledge. Each book became a steppingstone towards personal growth and enlightenment.

As I devoured the words on those pages, I realized the immense power of the written word. It ignited a fire within me, fueling my desire to learn, explore, and achieve greatness. These books had empowered me with the knowledge that education held the key to unlocking doors and overcoming the limitations imposed by my circumstances. The more I read, the more I yearned to expand my knowledge, to delve into new subjects, and to sharpen my intellect.

Those books were my constant companions throughout that period of my life, providing solace during challenging times and serving as a source of inspiration whenever I faced obstacles on my journey. They became the foundation upon which I built my dreams and aspirations, and I still owe a lot of my success to them today, Through the stories and lessons contained within those pages, I learned the importance of perseverance, resilience, and the relentless pursuit of my goals.

Now as much as ever, I carry the lessons learned from "Gifted Hands" and those treasured books along with me in my continued strive for excellence. They serve as a constant reminder that regardless of our circumstances, we have the power to shape our destinies. I am eternally grateful for the transformative impact they had on my life and the invaluable gift of a gifted mind they bestowed upon me.

IMPORTANCE OF NURTURING AND SUPPORTING GIFTED INDIVIDUALS

Gifted individuals possess exceptional intellectual abilities, intense curiosity, creativity, and high levels of motivation. By providing the necessary support and opportunities, we can unlock their full potential, cultivate their talents, and help them make significant contributions to society. Recognizing and nurturing these gifted minds is of paramount importance for several reasons. One of the key reasons for nurturing and supporting gifted individuals is to ensure that their unique abilities are not overlooked or wasted. Gifted individuals often possess advanced cognitive skills, a high IQ, and the ability to process information rapidly. If left unsupported or unchallenged, they may become disengaged, bored, or frustrated in traditional educational settings. This can lead to underachievement or a lack of fulfillment in their academic pursuits. Therefore, by recognizing their giftedness and providing appropriate, tailored educational interventions, we can ensure that their abilities are nurtured and developed to their fullest extent. After all, this may eventually benefit our society as a whole!

Additionally, nurturing gifted individuals is crucial because they possess an insatiable curiosity and a deep passion for learning. These individuals often exhibit a voracious appetite for knowledge and a desire to explore multiple subjects in-depth. By fostering an environment that encourages and supports their intellectual curiosity, we can fuel their love for learning and provide them with the intellectual stimulation they crave.

Moreover, supporting gifted individuals is essential for harnessing their creativity and divergent thinking. Gifted minds have a remarkable ability to generate unique and innovative ideas, think outside the box, and challenge conventional norms. As such, these individuals have the potential to revolutionize various fields, whether it be in the arts, sciences, technology, or entrepreneurship. By providing them with the necessary resources, mentorship, and opportunities, we empower gifted individuals to unleash their creativity and contribute to the advancement of society.

In addition to academic support, nurturing gifted individuals also requires attention to their social and emotional needs. Gifted individuals may experience feelings of isolation, intellectual loneliness, or a sense of being different from their peers. Providing social and emotional support is crucial for their overall well-being. Counseling, mentorship, and creating opportunities for peer interaction can help them connect with like-minded individuals, develop interpersonal skills, and build a strong support network.

Lastly, nurturing and supporting gifted individuals is essential for creating a more inclusive and equitable society. By recognizing and providing equal opportunities to gifted individuals from diverse backgrounds, we can break down barriers and ensure that talent is not limited by social, economic, or cultural factors. Nurturing gifted individuals from underrepresented communities can help bridge the achievement gap, promote diversity in various fields, and cultivate a more inclusive society where everyone has the chance to excel.

.

PERSONAL ENCOUNTER WITH THE BOOK "GIFTED HANDS" BY BEN CARSON

As I mentioned earlier, I was in my twenties—a period of self-discovery and exploration—when I first stumbled on the literary gem that would leave an indelible mark on my journey: *Gifted Hands*. As I held the book in my hands, its cover adorned with the image of a determined surgeon, I had no idea that within its pages lay a treasure trove of wisdom, inspiration, and the remarkable story of a man who defied all odds.

From the opening lines I found myself captivated by the raw and honest narrative that unfolded before me. Ben Carson's words resonated deep within my soul, as he recounted his struggles, setbacks, and triumphs with unwavering honesty and vulnerability. It was a story of determination, resilience, and the unwavering belief in the power of the human mind. As I delved deeper into the book, I found myself immersed in the awe-inspiring journey of Ben Carson. From his humble beginnings in inner-city Detroit to becoming one of the world's most renowned neurosurgeons, his path was not without obstacles. He faced poverty, discrimination, and self-doubt, but through it all, he held onto an unyielding belief in his own potential.

Through his story, I learned that greatness is not determined by one's circumstances, but by the choices we make and the relentless pursuit of excellence. Ben Carson's unwavering commitment to his craft, his unquenchable thirst for knowledge, and his unyielding work ethic were a testament to the power of dedication and determination. The book's title, "Gifted Hands," took on a deeper meaning as I progressed through the chapters. It became apparent that the true gift lay not only in the dexterity of Ben Carson's surgical hands but also in the extraordinary capabilities of his mind. It was through the cultivation of his mental faculties that he transformed his life and touched the lives of countless others.

The book challenged me to reflect on my own gifts and talents, urging me to uncover and nurture them. It reminded me that we are all born with unique abilities, bestowed upon us by a higher power, waiting to be discovered and utilized for the greater good. It was a call to action, urging me to channel my efforts and energy towards realizing my full potential. I responded to this urge and found that—by the time I read the book's poignant final words—there was a fire ignited within me, fueling my desire to break free from the limitations imposed by society, circumstances, and self-doubt.

The encounter with this remarkable book sparked a paradigm shift in my thinking. It shattered the self-imposed barriers of my mind and expanded the horizons of possibility. It instilled in me an unwavering belief that with dedication, perseverance, and a steadfast commitment to personal growth, I too could achieve greatness in my chosen path. "Gifted Hands" by Ben Carson not only gifted me with a compelling narrative but also with a roadmap for personal and professional success. It taught me the importance of discipline, hard work, and the pursuit of knowledge. It reminded me that the mind is a powerful instrument, capable of shaping our reality and transforming our lives.

In retrospect, I am immensely grateful for the fortuitous encounter with "Gifted Hands." It came into my life at a time when I needed guidance, inspiration, and a renewed sense of purpose. The book continues to hold a special place in my heart, serving as a constant reminder of the incredible potential residing within each one of us. It stands as a testament to the transformative power of literature and the profound impact that a single book can have on an individual's life.

THE PROFOUND IMPACT OF THE BOOK ON PERSONAL GROWTH AND MINDSET

From the moment I embarked on the journey of *Gifted Hands'* pages, my perspective on life, my aspirations, and my understanding of human potential were forever transformed. As I delved into the depths of the book, I was confronted with the remarkable story of a man who defied all odds and rose to greatness through sheer determination and unwavering belief in himself.

The book served as a wake-up call, shaking me out of my complacency and challenging me to explore the depths of my own potential. It shattered the preconceived limitations I had unknowingly imposed upon myself, urging me to reach for the stars and embrace the boundless possibilities that life had to offer. Ben Carson's unwavering determination and relentless pursuit of excellence fueled my own desire to cultivate a growth mindset, to constantly challenge myself, and to embrace the idea that failures are steppingstones to success.

Ben Carson's journey was not without its share of challenges, setbacks, and moments of self-doubt. Yet, he persisted, refusing to let obstacles define his path. This resonated deeply with me, inspiring me to develop a resilient mindset that would propel me forward even in the face of adversity. For the same reasons, "Gifted Hands" underscored the significance of lifelong learning and personal development. Ben Carson's voracious appetite for knowledge, his dedication to continuous improvement, and his unwavering commitment to honing his skills showcased the transformative power of education. It instilled in me a thirst for knowledge, a hunger to expand my horizons, and a deep appreciation for the transformative potential of learning.

The book also fostered a sense of responsibility within me. It reminded me that each of us possesses unique gifts and talents that can be utilized for the betterment of society. Ben Carson's journey exemplified the importance of using one's abilities not solely for personal gain, but for the greater good. It ignited a desire within me to contribute meaningfully to the world, to make a positive impact, and to leave a legacy.

Furthermore, "Gifted Hands" inspired me to challenge conventional wisdom and think beyond the boundaries of societal expectations. Ben Carson's story showcased the power of defying stereotypes, transcending limitations, and charting one's own path to success. It encouraged me to embrace my individuality, to embrace the unconventional, and to pursue my passions fearlessly.

"Gifted Hands" has left an indelible mark on my personal growth and mindset. Its profound message of resilience, determination, and the transformative power of the human mind continues to inspire me to this day. It has equipped me with the tools necessary to overcome challenges, embrace growth, and make a meaningful impact in the world. After you finish my book, I urge you—from the bottom of my heart—to find yourself a copy of Gifted Hands, and to let yourself get lost within its pages.

THE POWER OF THE MIND

The power of the mind is an awe-inspiring force that shapes our reality, determines our actions, and influences our overall well-being. It is the driving
engine behind our thoughts, emotions, and behaviors, and holds the key to
unlocking our full potential. As I contemplate the immense capabilities of
the human mind, I am astounded by its profound impact on every aspect of
our lives.

At its core, the mind is a complex and intricate web of neural networks,
constantly processing information, making connections, and generating
thoughts. It is a powerhouse of creativity, problem-solving, and innovation.
Through the power of imagination, the mind can conceive ideas that have the
potential to change the world.

One of the remarkable aspects of the mind is its remarkable ability to learn,
grow, and rewire itself based on new experiences and knowledge. This neuro-
plasticity allows us to develop new skills, overcome challenges, and reshape
our beliefs and attitudes. With conscious effort and practice, we can train our
minds to think more positively, cultivate resilience, and embrace a growth
mindset.

The mind is also the gateway to our emotions. It is through the mind that
we experience joy, love, happiness, as well as sadness, fear, and anger. Our
thoughts and perceptions shape our emotional landscape, influencing how
we interpret and respond to the world around us. By developing emotional
intelligence and cultivating mindfulness, we can harness the power of the
mind to cultivate positive emotions and navigate challenging situations with
grace and resilience.

The mind is not confined to the realm of the individual. It has the ability to
connect us with others, fostering empathy, understanding, and cooperation.
Through the power of empathy, the mind can bridge the gaps between diverse individuals and foster a sense of unity and compassion. It allows us to
recognize and appreciate the shared human experience, transcending differ-
ences and promoting harmonious relationships.

Furthermore, the mind holds the power to shape our physical health and
well-being. Research has shown that the mind-body connection is a powerful
phenomenon. Our thoughts and beliefs influence our immune system, stress

levels, and overall physical health. Through practices such as meditation, visualization, and positive affirmations, we can harness the power of the mind to promote healing, reduce stress, and enhance overall well-being.

The power of the mind extends beyond the individual level. Collectively, our minds have the potential to drive societal change, innovation, and progress. Throughout history, great minds have shaped the course of humanity through their ideas, inventions, and discoveries. From scientific breakthroughs to social movements, the collective power of minds coming together has transformed the world we live in.

However, with great power comes great responsibility. It is crucial that we understand the influence our minds have on our own lives and the lives of others. By cultivating self-awareness, we can become conscious of our thoughts, beliefs, and biases. This awareness empowers us to challenge limiting beliefs, embrace diversity, and promote positive change.

In conclusion, the power of the mind is an extraordinary phenomenon that shapes our perception, emotions, behaviors, and overall well-being. It is a force that has the potential to unlock our full potential, foster personal growth, and drive positive change in the world. By harnessing the power of our minds, we can embark on a transformative journey of self-discovery, resilience, and limitless possibilities.

THE INSPIRING JOURNEY OF BEN CARSON

Born into a challenging environment, Ben Carson faced numerous obstacles that could have easily deterred him from pursuing his dreams. However, fueled by the unwavering support of his mother and his own inner determination, he defied the odds and charted a path towards excellence.

One of the most remarkable aspects of Ben Carson's journey is his unyielding commitment to education and personal growth. Recognizing the transformative power of knowledge, he immersed himself in books, devouring their contents and expanding his horizons. His thirst for knowledge was insatiable, and he understood that education was the key to unlocking doors that had long been closed to him.

What sets Ben Carson apart is not just his professional accomplishments but also his commitment to giving back to society. Throughout his career, he has dedicated his time and expertise to improving the lives of others, particularly children facing medical challenges. His philanthropic efforts and advocacy for education have left an indelible impact on countless individuals and communities.

Moreover, Ben Carson's story is a testament to the importance of mentorship and support. Along his journey, he encountered individuals who believed in his potential and provided guidance and mentorship. These influences played a significant role in shaping his trajectory and instilling in him the confidence and determination to pursue his dreams.

Ben Carson's journey is a reminder that greatness lies within each of us, waiting to be awakened. It is a call to action, urging individuals to rise above their circumstances, embrace their unique gifts, and make a positive impact on the world. His story exemplifies the transformative power of determination, education, and unwavering belief in oneself.

UNLEASHING THE POTENTIAL OF GIFTED MINDS

Supporting gifted minds is a multifaceted and dynamic process that requires a comprehensive approach capable of addressing the unique needs and challenges of these individuals. Those with gifted minds possess truly exceptional intellectual abilities, intense curiosity, creativity, and motivation, making it essential to provide them with tailored educational opportunities, a nurturing environment, and social and emotional support.

One of the primary ways to support gifted minds is through educational enrichment programs. These programs offer advanced coursework, accelerated learning opportunities, and specialized curricula that cater to the intellectual capabilities and interests of gifted students. By challenging them with complex and in-depth material, these programs ensure that gifted minds are engaged and continuously expanding their knowledge base. They also provide an environment in which these individuals can interact with like-minded peers, fostering collaboration, intellectual discourse, and the exchange of ideas.

In addition to enrichment programs, individualized learning approaches play a crucial role in supporting gifted individuals. Recognizing that each gifted mind is unique, personalized learning allows for tailored instruction, flexible pacing, and the exploration of specific areas of interest. This approach ensures that gifted individuals receive the intellectual challenges they need while also having the freedom to delve more deeply into subjects they are passionate about. Mentoring from knowledgeable educators who understand the specific needs of gifted minds further enhances the learning experience and provides guidance for academic and personal growth.

Creating a nurturing environment is equally important for supporting gifted minds. Gifted individuals thrive in an environment that values and encourages intellectual exploration and expression. It is essential to establish a safe space where they can freely share their thoughts, ideas, and questions without fear of judgment or ridicule. Such an environment fosters a sense of belonging, encourages risk-taking, and nurtures their confidence and self-esteem. Furthermore, promoting collaboration among gifted individuals enables them to learn from one another, collaborate on projects, and engage in stimulating discussions that enhance their understanding and perspective.

Supporting the social and emotional well-being of gifted minds is vital for their overall development. Gifted individuals often face unique challenges, such as asynchronous development, heightened sensitivity, perfectionism, and feelings of isolation. Providing social and emotional support through counseling, mentorship, and peer interaction helps them navigate these challenges effectively. It allows them to develop coping mechanisms, resilience, and a healthy balance between their academic pursuits and personal well-being. Addressing their social and emotional needs not only enhances their overall happiness and satisfaction but also facilitates their continued intellectual growth and success.

To unleash the full potential of gifted minds, it is crucial to encourage multidisciplinary learning. Gifted individuals possess diverse interests and talents, and integrating various subjects allows for the exploration of connections and intersections between different fields. By engaging in multidisciplinary learning experiences, gifted individuals develop a broader perspective, gain a deeper understanding of complex issues, and cultivate creativity through the synthesis of ideas from different domains. This approach nurtures well-rounded individuals who can approach problems from multiple angles and contribute meaningfully to various disciplines.

Gifted individuals possess exceptional analytical abilities and the capacity for complex reasoning. Therefore, providing challenging tasks, open-ended problems, and opportunities to engage in real-world applications of their knowledge enhances their critical thinking and problem-solving abilities. By encouraging them to think critically, analyze information, evaluate evidence, and develop innovative solutions, we equip them with the tools necessary to address complex challenges and make a positive impact on society.

Lastly, supporting gifted minds involves inspiring leadership and encouraging these individuals to make a positive impact. Gifted people possess the potential to become influential leaders and change-makers. By providing opportunities for leadership development, fostering a sense of responsibility, and promoting community engagement, we empower them to use their talents to bring about positive change. Whether it is through innovative projects, advocacy, or mentoring others, supporting gifted minds in their leadership endeavors cultivates a sense of purpose, instills values of social consciousness, and helps them realize the impact they can have on the world.

Ultimately, unleashing the potential of gifted minds requires creating an environment that nurtures exploration, promotes a growth mindset, and provides opportunities for leadership and positive impact. By embracing multidisciplinary learning, fostering a belief in the power of effort and resilience, and empowering gifted individuals to make a difference, we unlock their full potential. Through their unique insights, creativity, and leadership, gifted minds have the capacity to shape a brighter future for themselves and contribute to the betterment of society.

CHAPTER ELEVEN
TIME

Time is a fascinating concept that plays an inherent, inescapable role in our lives. Elusive nature is a force that yields many emotions: Many of us desire an infinite amount of time, and many of us find ourselves continually regretting its passage. In many ways, time can be likened to valuable resources such as money or precious metals; It is something that carries an indelible impact on our existence, and it is, by and large, impossible to live a life free of its influence.

One of the remarkable, and often hurtful, aspects of time is its role in depreciating the value of our assets. As the clock ticks away, the value of our possessions, achievements, and relationships undergoes a transformation. Time becomes the measuring stick against which our accomplishments are assessed. It is a determining factor in evaluating the worth and growth of our financial investments, as well as a catalyst for predicting future outcomes.

Perhaps the most poignant reflections on the significance of time arise when we contemplate our relationships, particularly those we hold with family members and loved ones. Regrettably, we often only appreciate the value of time spent with these people when they are no longer with us. In the moments that we spend reflecting on the person we knew, it is natural that we find ourselves yearning for more time to create more memories, share more laughter, and strengthen the bonds that death or distance has abruptly severed. Yet we must strive to apply these lessons to our current lives, too – the passage of time can grant us the wisdom of understanding how important it is to truly cherish the moments we share with those dear to us.

Paradoxically, however, time is also susceptible to being squandered on trivial matters. We often find ourselves engaging in activities that offer little value or purpose, wasting precious moments that could have been used productively. This is an ever-increasing concern in the social media age, where applications with 'endless scroll' features make it easier than ever to get lost in our own bubble. The guilt that we may feel later serves as a stark reminder that time, unlike any other commodity, cannot be repurchased or regained once lost. It stands as a finite resource that demands careful consideration and conscientious allocation.

In the grand scheme of things, most individuals are bestowed with, roughly speaking, the same amount of time. It is the choices we make and the actions we take within that timeframe that truly count. How ferociously do we grasp the opportunity to mold our lives, pursue our passions, cultivate relationships, and leave a lasting impact on the world? This determines how valuable we make our time feel. The way we utilize our time is entirely within our own power, and it can determine the trajectory of our lives, with the memories we create becoming the priceless treasures that transcend its fleeting nature.

DEFINITION OF TIME AS A FUNDAMENTAL CONCEPT IN HUMAN EXISTENCE

As we have discussed, time, an ethereal phenomenon woven intricately into the fabric of our lives, stands as a fundamental concept in the tapestry of human existence. But what is time, really? At first glance, it may seem straightforward—a mere measurement of the duration between events. Yet, upon deeper reflection, time is revealed to be far more profound and enigmatic, something that transcends the realms of science and philosophy, captivating the minds of scholars, mystics, and dreamers alike.

In its essence, time is the vessel that carries our experiences, memories, and aspirations. It is the invisible thread that weaves together the past, present, and future, granting us the ability to navigate the realms of temporal existence. From the fleeting moments of joy to the profound sorrows, time is the canvas upon which our lives are painted. Beyond its practical implications, time encompasses a vast spectrum of meanings and interpretations. It embodies the ephemerality of youth, the wisdom accrued through aging, and the bittersweet nostalgia that accompanies the passage of years.

In our daily lives, time imposes deadlines and schedules, reminding us of the finite nature of our earthly sojourn. It urges us to seize the moment and make the most of the precious time we have been granted. After all, we have no guarantee regarding how long this may be. Still, time is not merely an abstract concept or a societal construct; It is something that resonates with us on a deeply personal level, evoking emotions and provoking introspection. It prompts us to reflect on the brevity of life and to contemplate the profound meaning hidden within the passing seconds, minutes, and hours.

THE SIGNIFICANCE OF TIME IN LIFE AND SOCIETY

Time holds a profound significance that permeates every aspect of our existence. From the personal realm to the grand tapestry of society, time weaves its influence, shaping our actions, molding our identities, and defining the very essence of our being.

In the realm of personal development, time stands as the ultimate arbiter of progress and growth. It is the currency through which we invest our efforts, talents, and aspirations. Every decision we make, every goal we set, is intrinsically linked to the passage of time. It serves as a constant reminder of our mortality, urging us to seize the moment and maximize the value of our limited stay on this Earth. Time serves as a mentor, guiding our learning, growth, and transformation. It presents us with opportunities to gain knowledge, cultivate skills, and enhance our talents, and grants us the wisdom that comes from both successes and challenges, nurturing our emotional intelligence and facilitating personal development.

Time is also a vital ingredient in cultivating connections, fostering intimacy, and building bonds that transcend the temporal realm. The time we invest in nurturing our relationships with loved ones, friends, and colleagues lays the foundation for trust, understanding, and shared experiences. This echoes the value of time on a societal level too, at which time serves as a powerful organizing principle, synchronizing the collective efforts of humanity. It provides the framework within which societies function, enabling coordination, planning, and progress. From the intricate choreography of transportation systems to the synchronized rhythms of economic activities, time dictates the pace and efficiency of societal functioning.

Finally, time acts as the currency of productivity and efficiency, driving inno-vation, and shaping the dynamics of work and labor. It impels us to prioritize tasks, allocate resources wisely, and optimize our efforts to achieve desired outcomes. In the workplace, effective time management fosters productivity, empowers individuals, and fuels collective progress. In art, culture, and en-tertainment, time is an essential dimension that artists harness to convey nar-ratives, evoke emotions, and captivate audiences. From the tempo of music to the pacing of storytelling, the manipulation of time immerses us in worlds created by the most creative minds that humanity has to offer.

UNDERSTANDING TIME MANAGEMENT

Time management is a skill and discipline that involves consciously and ef-fectively allocating and utilizing time to accomplish tasks, meet goals, and maintain a balanced and fulfilling life. It is an essential aspect of personal and professional success, allowing individuals to optimize productivity, re-duce stress, and make the most of their limited time.

At its core, time management revolves around the concept of prioritization. It requires individuals to identify and determine the importance and urgency of tasks and activities in order to allocate time accordingly. By prioritizing tasks, individuals can focus their energy and attention on the most signifi-cant and impactful activities, ensuring that they are working towards their goals and desired outcomes. Time management encompasses various funda-mental aspects. Let's break some of these down.

Setting Clear Goals:

Without clearly defined objectives, it becomes challenging to allocate time effectively and prioritize tasks. By establishing specific, measurable, achiev-able, relevant, and time-bound (SMART) goals, individuals can create a roadmap for their actions and identify the steps necessary to achieve those goals. Goals provide a sense of direction and purpose, guiding individuals in their decision-making and time allocation.

Planning and Scheduling

Planning and scheduling are vital components of effective time management. Developing a comprehensive plan involves breaking down larger goals into smaller, manageable tasks and identifying the necessary resources and time frames for each task. Scheduling involves allocating specific time slots to these tasks, creating a structured framework for daily, weekly, or monthly activities. This allows individuals to have a clear overview of their commitments, deadlines, and available time, minimizing the risk of overcommitment and ensuring that important tasks are not overlooked.

Prioritization and Time Allocation:

Prioritization and time allocation require individuals to differentiate between urgent and important tasks. Urgent tasks are those that require immediate attention due to impending deadlines or time-sensitive nature. Important tasks, on the other hand, are those that align with long-term goals, contribute to personal growth, or have significant consequences. While urgent tasks often demand immediate attention, it is crucial to not neglect important tasks in the process. Balancing both urgent and important tasks is essential for effective time management.

Elimination of Distractions:

Time wasters can come in various forms, such as excessive social media use, unnecessary meetings, or engaging in unproductive activities. Identifying these time wasters and implementing strategies to minimize or eliminate them can significantly enhance productivity and time utilization. This may include setting boundaries for technology use, practicing mindful work habits, or delegating tasks when appropriate.

Task Delegation:

A critical aspect of time management is the ability to delegate and outsource tasks. Recognizing when it is more efficient and effective to involve others in completing certain tasks can free up valuable time for more important responsibilities. Delegation allows individuals to focus on tasks that require their specific expertise and decision-making, while outsourcing tasks to professionals or utilizing technology can leverage specialized skills and resources.

Rest and Rejuvenation:

Overworking and neglecting self-care can lead to burnout and decreased productivity. Allocating time for relaxation, hobbies, physical exercise, and quality sleep is essential for maintaining energy levels, enhancing focus, and promoting overall well-being. Taking breaks throughout the day, practicing mindfulness, and engaging in activities that bring joy and relaxation contribute to sustained productivity and motivation.

Discipline:

Time management requires individuals to cultivate discipline and develop healthy work habits. This includes managing procrastination, setting realistic deadlines, and maintaining focus on tasks at hand. Techniques such as breaking down tasks into smaller, manageable parts, using timers or Pomodoro technique for focused work, and practicing self-accountability can help overcome procrastination and improve productivity.

THE BENEFITS OF TIME MANAGEMENT

- **Productivity and Achievement:** Effective time management enables us to prioritize tasks, set goals, and allocate time efficiently. By doing so, one can accomplish more within a given timeframe, leading to increased success and personal fulfillment.
- **Reduced Stress and Overwhelm:** Proper time management prevents us from feeling overwhelmed by our responsibilities and commitments. By organizing and prioritizing tasks, individuals can approach their workload in a structured and controlled manner, reducing stress and promoting a sense of calm.
- **Opportunities for Personal Growth:** Time management allows individuals to dedicate time to personal growth and self-improvement. It provides opportunities for learning, acquiring new skills, pursuing hobbies, and engaging in activities that contribute to personal development.
- **Work-Life Balance:** Balancing professional and personal commitments is essential for overall well-being and happiness. Time management helps individuals allocate appropriate time to work, family, relationships, leisure, and self-care, ensuring a harmonious and fulfilling life.

- **Efficiency and Effectiveness:** By managing time effectively, individuals can eliminate time-wasting activities, minimize distractions, and focus on tasks that yield the greatest results. This increased efficiency leads to higher effectiveness in both personal and professional endeavors. In an era characterized by constant connectivity and digital distractions, managing your time skillfully enables you to establish boundaries and create designated periods of uninterrupted work.

- **Goal Achievement:** Time management facilitates the alignment of actions with goals. By setting clear objectives, breaking them down into manageable steps, and allocating time for their completion, individuals can make consistent progress and achieve their desired outcomes.

- **Enhanced Decision-Making:** Time management enables individuals to make informed decisions by considering the time required, deadlines, and priorities associated with each choice. It promotes a more thoughtful and deliberate approach to decision-making, leading to better outcomes.

- **More Time Freedom:** One of the primary advantages derived from effective time management is the attainment of greater time freedom. When we have a sense of time freedom, we gain the ability to allocate our precious hours towards setting and accomplishing our most significant goals.

- **Quality Relationships:** Time management allows individuals to allocate dedicated time to nurturing and maintaining meaningful relationships. By balancing work and personal commitments, individuals can invest time in building strong connections with family, friends, and loved ones.

- **Overall Life Satisfaction:** Effective time management empowers individuals to take control of their lives and make intentional choices about how they spend their time. By aligning their actions with their values and priorities, individuals experience greater fulfillment, purpose, and satisfaction.

Overall, the benefits of managing time extend beyond mere productivity gains. By mastering the art of time management, you unlock the potential to accomplish significant results, reduce stress levels, and nurture deeper connections with your loved ones. Effectively managing your time empowers you to focus your energy on what truly matters, leading to a more purposeful and fulfilling life. This newfound freedom allows you to allocate more quality time to the people who hold significant importance in your life.

CHAPTER TWELVE
WELLNESS

Health is an integral aspect of overall well-being that significantly influences our ability to function optimally in every aspect of life. It encompasses not only physical well-being but also that relating to our mental, spiritual, and social health. Achieving complete health requires a holistic approach, where all aspects of one's being - mind, body, emotions, and spirit - harmoniously coexist.

Contrary to popular belief, being healthy is not solely about having a fit physique. It is equally important to nurture and maintain a sound state of mind. Emotional well-being plays a crucial role, requiring individuals to be attuned to their emotions and develop a sense of self-awareness. Additionally, taking care of one's body by keeping it active and well-nourished is vital. Engaging in regular exercise, even simply walking or cycling a few times a week, can bring a significant positive impact. Moreover, adopting a balanced and nutritious diet further contributes to overall well-being. Lastly, fostering a sense of belonging and purpose in one's spiritual being completes the holistic approach to achieving optimal health.

Wellness necessitates prioritizing health over materialistic pursuits, such as financial gain. Though it can be challenging to decline extra work hours when burdened with debts, it is crucial to recognize the potential adverse consequences of prioritizing money over health. Indeed, numerous empirical studies have revealed that excessive overtime work can have both short-term and long-term detrimental effects. Worryingly, fatigue resulting from prolonged work hours can increase the risk of workplace accidents, as individuals become tired and lose focus on their tasks. Furthermore, overworking has been linked to elevated blood pressure, as well as an increased susceptibility to stroke and heart disease.

As someone who previously worked as a Metro Transit bus driver for New York City Transit, I have firsthand knowledge of the detrimental effects of excessive overtime. During my time there, I heard many alarming accounts of the city's bus drivers enduring relentless 40-hour overtime weeks without any breaks. Shocking stories even emerged of drivers being unable to return home, and instead resorting to sleeping at the bus depot or in their cars. However, what often goes unnoticed is the tragic aftermath faced by a significant percentage of these drivers after retirement. Many succumbed to strokes within days or months of leaving their demanding jobs. Thus, being a bus driver is an inherently stressful occupation, with individuals enduring verbal abuse, physical assault, and constant harassment. Importantly, this shows that health issues are not limited to laborious manual work; the mental and physical ramifications of overworking can spread to employees in almost any occupation or position.

In conclusion, attaining complete health requires a comprehensive approach that prioritizes exercise, balanced nutrition, emotional self-care, and a sense of purpose. No matter how strong our financial urges may be, it is crucial to recognize the importance of wellness over monetary pursuits and the potential consequences of excessive overtime work. By prioritizing our health, we can strive for a more fulfilling and balanced life, promoting overall well-being and resilience.

IMPORTANCE OF PURSUING WELLNESS IN VARIOUS ASPECTS OF LIFE

In our fast-paced and demanding world, the significance of prioritizing wellness cannot be overstated. Taking proactive steps to maintain and enhance our wellness is not just a personal choice; it is an investment in a fulfilling and balanced life. Let us explore the compelling reasons why pursuing wellness across all aspects of life is of utmost importance.

Physical Wellness

Physical wellness is a fundamental aspect of our overall well-being, centered around the care and maintenance of our bodies. It encompasses adopting healthy habits, engaging in regular physical activity, nourishing our bodies, and ensuring adequate rest. I break these components down in more detail below. As you read through their descriptions, you might find it useful to consider how they apply to your own life.

- **Regular Exercise:** Engaging in regular exercise is a cornerstone of physical wellness. Regular exercise aids in improving cardiovascular health, boosting strength and flexibility, and enhancing overall fitness. Additionally, it contributes to weight management, reduces the risk of chronic diseases (such as heart disease, diabetes, and certain cancers), and promotes a healthy musculoskeletal system. Moreover, exercise releases endorphins, the "feel-good" hormones, which can elevate mood, reduce stress, and improve mental well-being.

- **Nourishing Our Bodies:** Proper nutrition plays a pivotal role in supporting physical wellness. A balanced diet that includes a variety of nutrient-dense foods fuels our bodies with the necessary vitamins, minerals, and macronutrients. Emphasizing whole grains, lean proteins, fruits, vegetables, and healthy fats ensures optimal nutrition. Adequate hydration is equally vital, aiding in digestion, the maintenance of body temperature, and the support of overall bodily functions. By making mindful choices about what we consume, we can provide our bodies with the fuel they need to thrive.

- **Rest and Recovery:** Sufficient sleep and rest is key for allowing the body to repair and rejuvenate. This is backed by an abundance of empirical stories showing that quality sleep can promote cognitive function, boost immunity, regulate hormone levels, and support our overall physical and mental health. Establishing a consistent sleep routine, creating a calming sleep environment, and practicing good sleep hygiene are essential for optimizing restorative sleep.

Incorporating Physical Wellness into your Daily Life

Integrating physical wellness practices into daily life is achievable through simple lifestyle adjustments. Prioritizing physical activity can be as simple as incorporating brisk walks during breaks, taking the stairs instead of the elevator, or participating in recreational activities that engage the body. Finding enjoyable forms of exercise, such as dancing, swimming, or cycling, increases the likelihood of maintaining consistency. Additionally, establishing healthy eating patterns by planning and preparing nutritious meals, limiting processed foods, and staying hydrated can lead to long-term positive outcomes.

For individuals with specific health concerns or those starting a new exercise regimen, it is highly recommended to seek guidance from healthcare professionals or certified fitness experts. These professionals can provide personalized advice and develop customized exercise and nutrition plans that consider individual needs, taking into account any underlying conditions or physical limitations. They possess valuable expertise in proper exercise techniques, injury prevention strategies, and appropriate nutrition to help individuals achieve their specific goals safely and effectively. Consulting with these professionals ensures that the exercise and nutrition plans are tailored to the individual's unique circumstances, promoting optimal health and well-being.

Physical wellness is a cornerstone of overall well-being, contributing to enhanced vitality, improved health, and a higher quality of life. By incorporating regular exercise, prioritizing proper nutrition, and ensuring adequate rest, individuals can reap the benefits of physical wellness, enabling us to fully enjoy life's experiences.

Mental Wellness

Mental wellness is a vital aspect of overall well-being, encompassing the state of one's emotional, psychological, and social health. It is the foundation for maintaining a balanced and fulfilling life, enabling individuals to cope with daily stressors, build resilience, and thrive in their personal and professional pursuits. Here are key elements to consider when focusing on mental wellness:

- **Self-awareness and Emotional Intelligence:** Developing self-awareness is essential in understanding and managing one's emotions effectively. By cultivating emotional intelligence, individuals can recognize and regulate their feelings, resulting in improved self-control, decision-making, and interpersonal relationships.

- **Stress Management:** Effective stress management techniques are crucial for mental wellness. This involves identifying stress triggers, implementing healthy coping mechanisms such as exercise, relaxation techniques, and time management strategies, and seeking support when needed.

- **Building Resilience:** Resilience is the ability to bounce back from adversity and cope with life's challenges. Developing resilience involves cultivating a positive mindset, nurturing strong support systems, fostering adaptability, and embracing personal growth opportunities.

- **Seeking Support:** Seeking support is a sign of strength, not weakness. It is important to reach out to trusted individuals, such as friends, family, or mental health professionals, when experiencing difficulties. Professional support can provide valuable guidance, tools, and perspectives to manage mental health concerns and promote overall well-being.

- **Work-Life Balance:** Achieving a healthy work-life balance is crucial for mental wellness. It involves setting boundaries between work and personal life, prioritizing self-care activities, and allocating time for relaxation, hobbies, and social connections. Balancing professional responsibilities with personal needs supports mental well-being and prevents burnout.

- **Mindfulness and Self-Care:** Practicing mindfulness and self-care can enhance mental wellness. Mindfulness involves being fully present in the moment, cultivating self-compassion, and engaging in activities that bring joy and relaxation. Likewise, delf-care activities, such as exercise, adequate sleep, healthy nutrition, and engaging in hobbies, promote mental and emotional well-being.

- **Building Positive Relationships:** Cultivating healthy connections with supportive individuals, fostering effective communication, and engaging in meaningful social interactions is essential for our mental wellness. Strong social connections provide a sense of belonging, support, and increased resilience against mental health challenges.

- **Reducing Stigma:** Promoting mental wellness requires actively combating the stigma surrounding mental health. Encouraging open conversations, education, and understanding can create supportive environments where individuals feel safe to seek help and share their experiences without fear of judgment or discrimination.

Prioritizing mental wellness is essential for improving overall quality of life, boosting productivity, and establishing a solid foundation for personal and professional success. By actively caring for our mental health, individuals not only benefit themselves but also contribute to the development of a compassionate and inclusive society that values the well-being of all its members. In the stressful and judgmental modern age, this can only be a good thing.

Emotional Wellness

Emotional wellness focuses on understanding and managing one's emotions effectively. It involves developing emotional intelligence, nurturing healthy relationships, and practicing self-care. Prioritizing emotional wellness allows individuals to navigate life's challenges with resilience and maintain a positive mental state. Below, we look at a few specific things you might wish to consider when assessing or improving your own emotional wellness.

- **Understanding Emotional Intelligence:** Emotional intelligence refers to the ability to recognize, understand, and manage one's own emotions, as well as empathize with the emotions of others. It involves self-awareness, self-regulation, social awareness, and relationship management. Cultivating emotional intelligence allows individuals to navigate interpersonal dynamics, resolve conflicts, and build stronger connections with others.

- **Managing Emotions:** Emotional wellness entails developing effective strategies to manage and regulate emotions. This includes recognizing and acknowledging a wide range of emotions, from joy and love to sadness and anger. By embracing emotions and understanding their underlying causes, individuals can respond to them in a healthy and constructive manner. Techniques such as mindfulness, deep breathing exercises, and journaling can help in managing emotions and promoting emotional well-being.

- **Building Resilience:** Resilience is the ability to bounce back from adversity, setbacks, and challenges. Emotional wellness involves cultivating resilience by developing coping mechanisms and adopting a growth mindset. This includes reframing negative thoughts, seeking support from trusted individuals, and learning from difficult experiences.

- **Nurturing Relationships:** Healthy relationships are vital for emotional well-being. Positive relationships provide a sense of belonging, emotional support, and opportunities for personal growth. Effective communication, active listening, empathy, and respect are essential components of nurturing healthy relationships.

- **Practicing Self-Care:** Self-care involves engaging in activities that promote self-nourishment and self-compassion. This can include setting boundaries, prioritizing personal needs, practicing relaxation techniques, pursuing hobbies and interests, and engaging in regular self-reflection. Taking time for oneself allows us to recharge, reduce stress, and maintain emotional balance.

- **Seeking Professional Help:** While we can take steps to enhance our own emotional well-being, it is essential to recognize when professional support may be needed. Mental health professionals can provide guidance, support, and evidence-based interventions to address specific emotional challenges. Seeking professional help is a proactive step towards emotional wellness and should be encouraged when necessary.

In summary, emotional wellness is a vital component of overall well-being. By understanding and managing emotions effectively, developing resilience, nurturing healthy relationships, practicing self-care, and seeking support when needed, individuals can cultivate emotional well-being and experience greater satisfaction in their lives. Prioritizing emotional wellness allows individuals to build inner strength, enhance their interpersonal relationships, and lead a more fulfilling and balanced life.

Social Wellness

Social wellness focuses on the quality and health of our relationships and interactions with others. It encompasses our ability to develop and maintain meaningful connections, build a support network, and contribute to the well-being of other individuals and society. Investing in social wellness can have a profound impact on our mental and emotional health, leading to increased happiness, reduced stress, and a greater sense of belonging. Again, let's explore some key elements of social wellness below.

- **Nurturing Healthy Relationships:** This involves cultivating connections with family, friends, colleagues, and acquaintances, based on mutual respect, trust, and support. Strong social bonds provide us with emotional support, encouragement, and a sense of belonging. They also contribute to our self-esteem and provide a network of individuals we can turn to during times of both joy and adversity.

- **Effective Communication:** Active listening, empathy, and clear expression of thoughts and emotions foster deeper connections with others. By actively engaging in conversations and understanding different perspectives, we enhance our relationships and promote mutual understanding and respect.

- **Conflict Resolution:** Conflict is a natural part of relationships, but learning healthy conflict resolution skills enables us to navigate disagreements with empathy and open-mindedness. By approaching conflicts as opportunities for growth and understanding, we can strengthen our relationships and create a harmonious social environment.

- **Community Engagement:** Being an active participant in

community initiatives, volunteering, or engaging in acts of kindness not only benefits others but also promotes a sense of purpose and fulfillment in our own lives. By supporting social causes, advocating for positive change, and promoting inclusivity and social justice, we contribute to the well-being of our communities and create a more equitable and supportive society.

- **Digital Health:** It is important to strike a balance between virtual and face-to-face interactions. While technology allows us to connect with others across vast distances, it is essential to prioritize meaningful in-person interactions. Spending quality time with loved ones, engaging in shared activities, and participating in social gatherings foster deeper connections and create lasting memories.

Social wellness plays a vital role in our overall well-being. Nurturing healthy relationships, practicing effective communication, resolving conflicts constructively, and actively engaging in our communities contribute to a fulfilling and meaningful social life. By investing in social wellness, we foster a sense of belonging, strengthen our support networks, and positively impact the lives of others. Prioritizing social wellness ultimately leads to a happier, more connected, and purposeful existence.

CHAPTER THIRTEEN
BALANCE

Balance is a crucial aspect of life, and Pastor Toure Roberts addresses this topic extensively in his insightful book, aptly titled *Balance*. The book resonated deeply with me, as many of the key points touched on aspects of my own life. I wholeheartedly recommend it to others seeking guidance in finding equilibrium. It is all too easy to become fixated on a single aspect of our lives, inadvertently neglecting other important areas. For some, the allure of money takes precedence, and when presented with the opportunity for overtime at work, they are the first to eagerly accept. Others may find themselves escaping from personal issues at home, leading them to readily sign up for extra shifts, inadvertently causing strain on their families. At one point, I, too, fell into this trap, believing that my loved ones should be grateful for the financial stability I was providing. I used to justify my absence by emphasizing the material possessions we could afford, or the occasional vacations we could enjoy. However, I failed to recognize that what children truly value is not the material things we buy for them but the quality time we spend together. It is imperative that we learn to prioritize what truly matters to us and allocate dedicated time for each aspect of our lives.

Learning to say "no" is, therefore, an essential habit that we must cultivate in order to achieve a balanced life. I used to be a chronic people-pleaser, and although I have made progress, remnants of that behavior still linger. My wife used to question why I would always rush to help others whenever they called, while unintentionally neglecting our own family's needs. Of course, it is not inherently wrong to assist others, but we must always do so with a strong sense of balance. Additionally, I have learned from experience that being too accommodating can jeopardize one's business. There were instances where I allowed my employees to take advantage of my kindness. For instance, I would rearrange work schedules to accommodate an employee's educational pursuits, only for them to quit abruptly later without providing sufficient notice to find a replacement.

Achieving balance in life requires conscious effort and a reevaluation of our priorities. Pastor Toure Roberts' book serves as an invaluable resource in navigating this journey. It highlights the importance of dedicating time to different aspects of our lives, such as our financial well-being, family relationships, and personal health. Furthermore, it underscores the significance of setting boundaries and learning to say "no" when necessary. By striking a harmonious balance, we can lead more fulfilling lives and nurture the relationships that matter most to us.

THE IMPORTANCE OF BALANCE IN LIFE

Balance refers to the state of equilibrium, harmony, and proportion between different elements. Whether it's physical, mental, emotional, or social well-being, finding the right balance is essential for overall happiness, success, and personal growth. Let's explore the significance of balance in different areas of life:

- **Work-Life Balance:** Striking a healthy work-life balance is vital for maintaining overall well-being. It involves allocating appropriate time and energy to work responsibilities while also nurturing personal relationships, pursuing hobbies, and taking care of oneself. Maintaining this equilibrium prevents burnout, reduces stress, enhances productivity, and fosters a fulfilling personal life.
- **Physical Health:** Balance in physical health encompasses maintaining a healthy diet, engaging in regular exercise, and getting enough rest and sleep. Balancing these elements ensures optimal functioning of the body, improves energy levels, boosts immunity, and reduces the risk of chronic illnesses. Neglecting any of these aspects can lead to physical imbalances and health issues.
- **Mental and Emotional Health:** Achieving balance in mental and emotional well-being involves managing stress, practicing self-care, nurturing positive relationships, and seeking support when needed.

It entails maintaining emotional stability, cultivating resilience, and finding inner peace. Balancing these aspects promotes mental clarity, emotional intelligence, and overall psychological well-being. Remember, you can back at Chapter 12 for further information on this.

- **Relationships:** Balance is crucial in maintaining healthy relationships. It involves giving and receiving support, practicing effective communication, respecting boundaries, and finding a middle ground. Balancing individual needs with the needs of others fosters harmonious relationships built on trust, mutual understanding, and empathy.

- **Personal Development:** Striving for balance in personal growth means allocating time and effort to various areas of self-improvement. It involves setting goals and priorities in areas such as career, education, hobbies, and personal interests. By maintaining a balanced approach, individuals can experience holistic personal development and avoid neglecting important aspects of their lives.

- **Financial Stability:** Balance in financial matters is crucial for long-term stability and security. It involves managing income, expenses, savings, and investments wisely. Striking a balance between spending and saving ensures financial independence, reduces stress, and provides a sense of security for the future.

- **Leisure and Recreation:** Balancing work and responsibilities with leisure and recreation is essential for rejuvenation and maintaining a positive outlook on life. Engaging in activities that bring joy, relaxation, and fulfillment helps individuals' recharge and prevent the negative effects of overworking or monotony.

By striving for balance, individuals can achieve a sense of harmony, fulfillment, and well-being. It allows for the integration of various elements, promotes self-awareness, and enhances overall quality of life. Embracing balance helps individuals lead healthier, happier, and more meaningful lives.

THE CONSEQUENCES OF IMBALANCE

Imbalance, whether in the physical, social, or emotional realms, often leads to various consequences that can have far-reaching effects. From individual well-being to global stability, the repercussions of imbalance can be significant and multifaceted. Let's take a brief look through some of the most common consequences of imbalance.

❖ **Health consequences:** In the realm of physical health, imbalance can manifest in different ways. Poor diet and lack of exercise can lead to obesity and chronic conditions such as heart disease and diabetes. Imbalance in sleep patterns can cause sleep disorders and impact cognitive function. Additionally, hormonal imbalances can disrupt bodily systems and contribute to various health issues.

❖ **Environmental degradation:** Imbalance between human activities and the natural environment can lead to severe ecological consequences. Uncontrolled deforestation, pollution, and excessive carbon emissions disrupt ecosystems, deplete biodiversity, and accelerate climate change. These imbalances contribute to the loss of habitats, species extinction, and the alteration of delicate ecological balances. The resulting environmental degradation not only threatens the health of the planet but also poses risks to human societies that depend on healthy ecosystems for resources and stability.

❖ **Social unrest:** Societal imbalances, such as economic inequality and social injustice, can give rise to social unrest and instability. When a significant portion of the population faces poverty, lacks access to education, and faces limited opportunities, it can lead to social dissatisfaction and unrest. Economic disparities can deepen divisions between different socioeconomic groups, fostering resentment and eroding social cohesion. This imbalance can lead to protests, conflicts, and even revolutions as marginalized groups demand fairness and equality.

❖ **Mental health issues:** Imbalance in mental and emotional well-being can have profound consequences on individuals and communities. Stress, anxiety, and depression can arise from a lack of balance between work, personal life, and self-care. Social isolation, another consequence of imbalance, can lead to feelings of loneliness and contribute to mental health issues. Moreover, the imbalance between societal expectations and individual values can create internal conflicts and identity crises, further impacting mental health.

❖ **Economic instability:** Imbalances in economic systems can lead to economic instability at various levels. When markets are characterized by excessive speculation, unequal distribution of wealth, or unsustainable debt levels, it can lead to financial crises, unemployment, poverty, and a decline in living standards, affecting individuals and communities alike. Economic imbalances between nations, such as trade deficits or currency fluctuations, can also cause disruptions in global markets and impact international relations.

❖ **Geopolitical tensions:** Imbalance in power dynamics between nations can contribute to geopolitical tensions and conflicts. When one nation or a group of nations holds significantly more economic, political, or military power than others, it can create an imbalance that leads to rivalries, aggression, and territorial disputes. The pursuit of dominance in such situations can result in regional conflicts, arms races, and even wars, with consequences that can be devastating for both the involved parties and the global community.

Addressing imbalances requires awareness, collective action, and policy interventions at various levels. By striving for balance in our personal lives, societies, and global systems, we can mitigate the consequences and work towards a more harmonious and sustainable world.

FINDING BALANCE IN FINANCES

Finding balance in finances is a crucial aspect of achieving financial well-being and maintaining a healthy relationship with money. It involves effectively managing your income, expenses, savings, and investments to ensure stability and avoid unnecessary stress. Here are some key principles to consider when seeking balance in finances.

- **Budgeting:** Creating and adhering to a budget is essential for managing your money effectively. It allows you to allocate funds to different categories such as housing, transportation, groceries, entertainment, and savings. By tracking your expenses and income, you can ensure that you're not overspending in one area while neglecting others.

- **Prioritizing Needs vs. Wants:** Distinguishing between needs and wants is crucial for maintaining balance in finances. Identify your essential expenses, such as food, shelter, utilities, and healthcare, and prioritize them over discretionary spending. By understanding the difference between what you need and what you want, you can make wiser financial decisions and avoid unnecessary debt.

- **Saving for Emergencies:** Building an emergency fund is a vital component of financial balance. Life is unpredictable, and having a safety net can help you navigate unexpected expenses, such as medical bills or job loss, without resorting to debt. Aim to save three to six months' worth of living expenses in a separate, easily accessible account.

- **Debt Management:** Balancing your finances requires effectively managing debt. While some debts may be necessary or justifiable, it's crucial to avoid excessive borrowing and high-interest debt. Decide to pay off outstanding debts systematically, starting with those with the highest interest rates. Minimizing and eventually eliminating debt will provide more financial freedom and flexibility.

- **Investing and Saving for the Future:** Achieving balance in finances also involves planning for the long term. Set financial goals, such as saving for retirement, buying a home, or starting a business, and develop an investment strategy to help you reach those goals. Consider diversifying your investments across different asset classes to mitigate risk.

- **Practicing Mindful Spending:** Mindful spending entails being conscious of how you allocate your money and ensuring that it aligns with your values and long-term goals. Before making a purchase, ask yourself if it adds genuine value to your life or if it's merely a temporary impulse. By practicing mindful spending, you can avoid unnecessary expenses more effectively.

- **Seeking Professional Guidance:** If you find it challenging to manage your finances or need help developing a comprehensive financial plan, consider seeking advice from a financial planner or advisor. They can provide valuable insights, help you set realistic goals, and guide you towards achieving financial balance.

Remember that finding balance in finances is a continuous process that requires regular evaluation and adjustments. It's essential to regularly review your financial situation, reassess your goals, and adapt your strategies as necessary. With diligence, discipline, and a commitment to making informed choices, you can achieve financial balance and secure a brighter future.

BALANCING WORK AND PERSONAL LIFE

Balancing work and personal life is a topic of immense importance in today's fast-paced and demanding world. As individuals, we often find ourselves caught up in the whirlwind of our professional obligations, constantly striving to meet deadlines, achieve targets, and advance our careers. However, it is equally vital to recognize the significance of maintaining a healthy work-life balance to ensure overall well-being, happiness, and fulfillment.

Work-life balance refers to the equilibrium between the time and effort we dedicate to our professional endeavors and the time we allocate to personal pursuits, family, friends, hobbies, self-care, and relaxation. It involves establishing boundaries, setting priorities, and making conscious choices to create a harmonious coexistence between work and personal life. There are several essential factors to consider when striving for work-life balance. Let's create a sort of step-by-step guide below.

1. First and foremost, it is crucial to define and understand one's personal values, goals, and priorities. This self-reflection enables individuals to identify what truly matters to them, helping them make informed decisions about how they allocate their time and energy.

2. Effective time management plays a pivotal role in achieving work-life balance. Prioritizing tasks, setting realistic goals, and creating a structured schedule can enhance productivity and prevent work from encroaching upon personal time. Employing tools such as calendars, to-do lists, and time-tracking apps can assist in organizing responsibilities and ensure that both work and personal commitments are met.

3. Establishing clear boundaries between work and personal life is another crucial aspect. This entails setting specific working hours and adhering to them, avoiding the temptation to constantly check emails or engage in work-related activities outside of designated work time. Likewise, it involves carving out dedicated time for personal activities, relaxation, and spending quality time with loved ones.

4. Open communication and effective delegation of tasks are essential for maintaining work-life balance, especially in the workplace. Being transparent about one's priorities and limitations with colleagues and superiors can foster understanding and cooperation, allowing for more flexible arrangements when necessary. Delegating tasks and seeking support when overwhelmed can prevent excessive workloads and reduce stress.

As you work your way through this plan, there are some things that you might do well to keep note of:

- Technology, although it can blur the line between work and personal life, can also be harnessed to promote work-life balance. Utilizing tools like email filters, automatic replies, and work collaboration platforms can streamline work processes, enhance efficiency, and provide greater flexibility in managing work responsibilities.

- Self-care and well-being should not be neglected when striving for work-life balance. Engaging in regular physical exercise, maintaining a healthy diet, getting sufficient sleep, and practicing mindfulness and relaxation techniques can significantly contribute to overall well-being, reduce stress levels, and increase productivity in both personal and professional life.

- Employers also play a crucial role in promoting work-life balance among their employees. Encouraging a culture that values work-life balance, implementing flexible working arrangements, providing resources for stress management, and fostering a supportive and inclusive work environment are instrumental in helping individuals maintain equilibrium and perform at their best.

Ultimately, achieving work-life balance is a continuous process that requires ongoing effort, self-awareness, and adaptability. It is not about completely separating work from personal life, but rather finding a sustainable and fulfilling integration of both domains. By recognizing the importance of work-life balance and actively implementing strategies to achieve it, individuals can lead more enriching, satisfying, and well-rounded lives.

OVERCOMING CHALLENGES AND MAINTAINING BALANCE

Overcoming challenges and maintaining balance in our lives is a constant journey that requires resilience, adaptability, and a commitment to self-care. Life is full of unexpected twists and turns, and navigating through obstacles can sometimes disrupt our sense of balance. However, with the right mindset and strategies, we can overcome challenges and find equilibrium in our lives. One of the key elements in overcoming challenges and maintaining balance is cultivating a positive and resilient mindset. Challenges are a natural part of life and viewing them as opportunities for growth and learning can help us approach them with a sense of optimism. Embracing a growth mindset allows us to interpret setbacks as temporary and not indicative of our worth or capabilities. Instead, we can focus on the lessons learned and use them to propel us forward.

Another essential aspect of maintaining balance is setting realistic goals and priorities. When faced with challenges, it is important we must assess our current situation and identify what truly matters to us. By prioritizing our goals, we can allocate our time, energy, and resources more effectively. This involves learning to say no to nonessential commitments and focusing on activities that align with our values and long-term vision. By managing our time and resources wisely, we can prevent overwhelming and maintain a healthier balance in our lives.

Effective stress management techniques play a crucial role in overcoming challenges and maintaining balance. Stress is an inevitable part of life, but we can control how we respond to the stressors we encounter. Engaging in regular exercise, such as yoga, meditation, or other relaxation techniques, can help reduce stress and promote mental and emotional well-being. Moreover, taking breaks, sleeping well, and incorporating self-care activities into our daily routine is essential for recharging our batteries and preventing burnout, bolstering our overall resilience and fostering an ability to face challenges head-on.

In addition to individual strategies, seeking support from others is vital in overcoming challenges and maintaining balance. Building a strong support network of friends, family, or mentors can provide us with encouragement, guidance, and perspective. Sometimes, talking through our challenges with someone we trust can help us gain clarity and new insights. When support from friends and family does not suffice, seeking help from qualified therapists or coaches can provide us with the tools and strategies needed to navigate specific challenges and maintain balance in our lives. There is no shame in seeking help (as we will discuss further in the following, penultimate chapter on our journey together).

Life is unpredictable, and being open to change and adjusting our plans when necessary is crucial. Embracing a flexible mindset allows us to adapt to new circumstances, seek alternative solutions, and bounce back from setbacks. It's important to remember that balance is not a fixed destination but rather an ongoing process that requires constant adjustment and recalibration.

Let your takeaway message from this section be this: overcoming challenges and maintaining balance in our lives is a continuous journey that requires resilience, adaptability, and self-care. By cultivating a positive mindset, setting realistic goals and priorities, managing stress effectively, seeking support, and embracing flexibility, we can navigate through obstacles and maintain a healthier balance in our lives. Remember, success is not about avoiding challenges but rather building the inner strength and strategies to overcome them and grow from the experience.

CHAPTER FOURTEEN
MENTAL HEALTH

The topic of mental health holds a special place in my heart due to its prevalence within my family. Having personally witnessed the impact that mental heath struggles can have on individuals, I have come to understand the havoc it can wreak. My academic exploration of this topic dates back to my undergraduate psychology courses, through which I gained valuable insights that reinforced the belief that every experience in life serves a purpose. Indeed, at the time, I had no idea that psychology would hold any practical significance for me. While I am not a professional in this field, I can comfortably declare that my research, personal experiences within my family, and past courses have equipped me with the ability to shed light on this important topic. As a disclaimer, though, I encourage you to access all the available resources if you feel that you may be able to benefit from the support we discuss in this section.

In the earlier chapters, we delved into the diverse mindsets that can detrimentally affect our financial well-being. Now, let us embark on an exploration of mental health and its profound influence on our overall wellness. It is no coincidence that we encounter individuals, whether on the streets or within psychiatric wards, who are grappling with mental health challenges. While certain forms of mental illness can be attributed to familial inheritance, akin to other physical ailments, it is crucial to acknowledge that—for most conditions—preventative measures can be taken to mitigate their occurrence.

One significant factor contributing to mental health issues is the overwhelming burden we place on our minds, be it through shouldering an excessive load of responsibilities or enduring the traumas life presents us. Furthermore, chronic worry exacerbates the risk of mental distress, potentially giving rise to feelings of depression or even more severe psychiatric conditions. It is imperative for individuals to cultivate the skill of minimizing worry concerning circumstances they have no control over.

Earlier on, we explored the detrimental effects of prolonged working hours on the physical aspect of our bodies. However, it is equally essential to address the toll it takes on our mental health. The act of dedicating extensive periods to work is a key driver of amplified stress levels. This heightened stress not only endangers our mental well-being, but also elevates the susceptibility to developing conditions such as depression, anxiety, and other mental health disorders. Hence, it is crucial for individuals to prioritize leisure time during weekends and strive to partake in at least one annual vacation, or ideally two if their financial circumstances permit.

Interestingly, the Bible itself emphasizes the significance of rest and rejuvenation. It recounts how even God, considered by many to be the omnipotent Creator of our world, set aside a day for rest after the arduous task of creation. This serves as a poignant reminder of the importance of incorporating periods of rest and relaxation into our lives to maintain optimal mental health. By recognizing the value of rest and making it a priority, we can nurture our mental well-being and strive for a healthier, more balanced existence.

DEFINITION OF MENTAL HEALTH

'Mental health' is a phrase that we hear increasingly often in modern society. But some people may still question what this means. In short, mental health refers to a person's emotional, psychological, and social well-being. It encompasses how individuals think, feel, and behave, as well as their ability to cope with stress, handle everyday challenges, build and maintain relationships, and make decisions. Good mental health means having a positive sense of self, experiencing a range of emotions in a healthy way, and being able to form and maintain meaningful relationships, even during times of adversity. Mental health affects all aspects of life, including how we think, feel, and act, and influences our ability to make choices and achieve our goals.

Mental health conditions or mental illnesses are disorders that can affect a person's thinking, mood, behavior, and daily functioning. Common examples include depression, anxiety disorders, bipolar disorder, schizophrenia, and post-traumatic stress disorder (PTSD). These conditions can vary in severity, but all can have a significant impact on a person's well-being, relationships, and overall quality of life.

It is important to note that good mental health is not solely about the absence of mental illness. Just as physical health exists on a continuum from good to poor, mental health also exists on a spectrum, and everyone falls somewhere along it. Taking care of our mental health involves adopting strategies and practices to promote emotional well-being, manage stress, seek support when needed, and maintain a healthy balance in various aspects of life.

UNDERSTANDING MENTAL HEALTH

Just like physical health, mental health can vary from good to poor, and it's position on the spectrum can fluctuate throughout a person's lifetime (or even from day-to-day). It is important to note that experiencing mental health challenges does not indicate weakness or a lack of character; Mental health issues can affect anyone, regardless of age, gender, race, or socioeconomic status. Many prominent celebrities, businesspeople and politicians—in other words, people who society regards as highly successful and desirable—have been vocal about their own struggles with mental health conditions. Use this as inspiration: there is no shame in suffering.

One common misconception about mental health is that it solely refers to mental illnesses or disorders. While mental illnesses are indeed a significant component of mental health, mental health encompasses a broader perspective. It also includes emotional well-being, resilience, coping mechanisms, and the ability to maintain positive relationships and handle the stresses of daily life.

Promoting good mental health involves fostering positive mental well-being, preventing mental illnesses, and supporting individuals with mental health challenges. It starts with recognizing the importance of self-care and making efforts to maintain good mental health. This can involve engaging in activities that bring joy and relaxation, seeking social support, practicing stress management techniques, and prioritizing healthy habits such as exercise, adequate sleep, and a balanced diet.

However, mental health issues can still arise despite one's best efforts to maintain good mental well-being. Mental illnesses such as depression, anxiety disorders, bipolar disorder, schizophrenia can affect individuals no matter how much they fight against it, and professional intervention and treatment is often required (and encouraged). Understanding mental health also means recognizing the signs and symptoms of mental illnesses, supporting individuals in seeking help, and reducing the stigma associated with mental health challenges.

Seeking professional help is crucial for individuals facing mental health difficulties. Mental health professionals, such as psychologists, psychiatrists, counselors, and therapists, are trained to provide support, guidance, and evidence-based treatments to those in need. Treatment may involve therapy, medication, or a combination of both tailored to the individual's specific needs.

Creating a society that understands and prioritizes mental health requires education, awareness, and stigmatization. It involves promoting open discussions about mental health, encouraging individuals to seek help when needed, and providing accessible mental health services. Furthermore, workplaces, schools, and communities can play a vital role in supporting mental health by implementing policies and programs that foster well-being and reduce stressors. This is an ongoing process, and one that has seen pleasing development in recent decades. Understanding mental health requires a shift in societal attitudes, increased support systems, and a commitment to promoting mental well-being. By acknowledging the significance of mental health, we can create a world that not only values physical health but also recognizes the importance of emotional and psychological well-being for individuals to thrive and lead fulfilling lives.

THE IMPORTANCE OF MENTAL HEALTH IN OVERALL WELL-BEING

The importance of mental health in our overall well-being cannot be overstated. Just as physical health is essential for a healthy body, mental health is crucial for a healthy mind. They are interconnected and influence each other in profound ways. When our mental health is compromised, it can have significant detrimental effects on our physical health and overall quality of life. Let's explore some of the fundamental reasons as to why striving to maintain good mental health is so important.

Daily Functioning

Good mental health allows us to think clearly, focus, and concentrate on tasks, which enhances productivity and performance in various areas of life, including work, studies, and personal relationships. On the other hand, poor mental health can lead to difficulties in concentration, memory, decision-making, and problem-solving, hindering our ability to function effectively.

Relationships and Social Interactions

Mental health also plays a crucial role in our relationships and social interactions. When we are mentally well, we are more likely to have healthy and fulfilling relationships, communicate effectively, and build strong social connections. Conversely, when our mental health suffers, it can lead to problems in our relationships, isolation, and feelings of loneliness.

Emotional Well-being

Furthermore, mental health is closely tied to our emotional well-being. It affects our ability to manage and regulate our emotions, handle stress, and cope with adversity. Good mental health enables us to experience and express a wide range of emotions in a healthy and balanced manner. It allows us to navigate life's ups and downs, bounce back from setbacks, and maintain resilience in the face of challenges.

Long-Term Consequences

Neglecting mental health can have severe long-term consequences, leading to the development or exacerbation of mental illnesses such as depression, anxiety disorders, bipolar disorder, and otters if not addressed over time. These conditions can significantly impact our long-term future, impairing our ability to work, study, maintain relationships, and enjoy life to its fullest. Acting today can help to avoid these long-term threats.

PROMOTING GOOD MENTAL HEALTH

Promoting mental health is a proactive approach that involves various strategies and practices. It includes practicing self-care, engaging in activities that bring joy and fulfillment, maintaining a healthy work-life balance, getting enough restful sleep, eating a balanced diet, exercising regularly, and managing stress effectively. Seeking support from loved ones, friends, or professionals is also crucial, helping us to create a supportive network and ensures access to appropriate care and treatment.

Society benefits from prioritizing mental health. When individuals are mentally healthy, they are more likely to contribute positively to their communities, engage in meaningful work, and build strong social connections. It can lead to increased productivity, creativity, and innovation, benefiting not only individuals but also the overall economy and social fabric.

As mentioned, there has been a growing recognition of the importance of mental health in recent years, leading to increased efforts to reduce stigma, raise awareness, and improve access to mental health services. However, much work still needs to be done. It is crucial for individuals, communities, governments, and organizations to continue promoting mental health, advocating for adequate resources and support, and ensuring that mental health is integrated into all aspects of healthcare. By investing in mental health, we can build a happier, more resilient, and thriving society.

THE PREVALENCE OF MENTAL HEALTH CONDITIONS

The prevalence of mental health issues is a growing concern worldwide. Mental health encompasses a wide range of conditions that affect a person's emotional, psychological, and social well-being. These conditions can have a profound impact on individuals, families, and communities, and addressing them is crucial for overall health and well-being. According to the World Health Organization (WHO), mental health disorders affect approximately one in four people at some point in their lives. This statistic highlights the significant burden that mental health issues place on individuals and societies. It is important to note that mental health issues can affect anyone, regardless of age, gender, socioeconomic status, or cultural background.

Various factors contribute to the prevalence of mental health issues. One key aspect is the complex interaction between genetic, biological, and environmental factors. Certain genetic predispositions can increase a person's susceptibility to mental health conditions, but environmental triggers and life experiences also play a crucial role in the development of these issues. Adverse childhood experiences, trauma, chronic stress, social isolation, discrimination, and poverty are just a few examples of factors that can significantly impact mental health, particularly for those individuals who hold a genetic predisposition to certain conditions. Let's break this down further:

1. **Biological Factors**

    - **Genetic predisposition:** Certain genetic factors can increase the susceptibility to mental health disorders. Family history of mental illnesses like depression, anxiety, or bipolar disorder can play a role.
    - **Neurochemical imbalances:** Imbalances in brain chemicals (neurotransmitters) such as serotonin, dopamine, and norepinephrine can affect mood regulation and contribute to mental health problems.
    - **Physical health conditions:** Chronic physical illnesses, hormonal imbalances, or neurological disorders can impact mental health. For instance, thyroid disorders or neurological conditions like Parkinson's disease may have associated mental health symptoms.

1. **Environmental Factors**

    - **Traumatic experiences:** Exposure to traumatic events like abuse, neglect, violence, or accidents can significantly impact mental health. Post-Traumatic Stress Disorder (PTSD) can develop as a result of such experiences.
    - **Childhood experiences:** Adverse childhood experiences (ACEs), such as parental divorce, abuse, neglect, or parental mental illness, can increase the risk of mental health issues later in life.
    - **Socioeconomic factors:** Poverty, unemployment, housing instability, or social inequality can contribute to chronic stress and negatively affect mental health.
    - **Social support:** Lack of strong social support systems or isolation can contribute to feelings of loneliness, depression, and anxiety.

1. Psychological Factors

- **Personality traits:** Certain personality traits, such as perfectionism, low self-esteem, or high levels of anxiety, can increase vulnerability to mental health problems.
- **Cognitive patterns:** Negative thinking patterns, distorted beliefs, and poor coping mechanisms can contribute to the development or exacerbation of mental health issues.
- **Traumatic or stressful life events:** Major life changes, loss of a loved one, relationship difficulties, or work-related stress can impact mental health.

Common mental health disorders include anxiety disorders, mood disorders (such as depression and bipolar disorder), personality disorders, psychotic disorders (such as schizophrenia), and eating disorders. These conditions can manifest in a range of symptoms, including persistent sadness, anxiety, irritability, changes in appetite and sleep patterns, difficulty concentrating, and thoughts of self-harm or suicide. The COVID-19 pandemic further exacerbated the prevalence of mental health issues. The isolation, fear, loss, and economic hardships caused by the pandemic have had a significant impact on people's mental well-being. Studies have reported an increase in anxiety, depression, and post-traumatic stress disorder (PTSD) symptoms among individuals affected by the pandemic, and this is a topic currently garnering a great deal of research in the relevant academic fields.

The prevalence of mental health issues is not limited to any region or country. It is a global phenomenon affecting people from all walks of life. However, the availability and accessibility of mental health services vary significantly worldwide. Many individuals with mental health conditions face barriers to accessing proper diagnosis, treatment, and support due to factors such as stigma, inadequate resources, and a shortage of mental health professionals.

Addressing the prevalence of mental health issues requires a comprehensive approach. It involves promoting mental health literacy and awareness to reduce stigma, improving access to mental health services, and integrating mental health care into primary health care systems. Education and awareness campaigns can help individuals recognize early signs of mental health issues and seek timely support. Governments and healthcare systems need to invest in mental health infrastructure, including trained professionals, facilities, and evidence-based treatments.

It's important to note that mental health problems are complex and often result from a combination of these factors. The interplay between biological, environmental, and psychological factors can vary from person to person, making everyone's experience unique. Understanding these contributing factors can help inform effective prevention, intervention, and treatment strategies to support mental well-being.

CHAPTER FIFTEEN
RETIREMENT

In the never-ending cycle of work, earning, and spending, we often neglect the crucial aspect of preparing for our future. Regrettably, the prevailing mindset among individuals revolves around immediate gratification, leading us to disregard the notion of paying ourselves first. Instead, we allocate our hard-earned money towards fulfilling the needs and demands of others, inadvertently disregarding our own financial well-being. Consequently, the concept of having a well-considered retirement plan often eludes us.

Indeed, a vast majority of people find themselves tragically ill-prepared for retirement, with dire financial consequences looming over their heads. As a result, the prospect of retirement becomes a distant dream, as the fear of destitution and homelessness instead grips their hearts. We frequently hear distressing anecdotes, such as that of an elderly lady resorting to eating cat food or an individual forced to go without important medications due to insufficient funds. These stories serve as poignant reminders of the urgent need to address the topic of retirement planning.

To shed light on this critical subject, let us delve into the realm of retirement plans. Firstly, we must familiarize ourselves with the renowned *401K plan*, which is a retirement savings account commonly offered by employers. Similarly, we must explore the concept of a pension—a defined benefit plan provided by certain companies to their employees, ensuring a steady income during retirement. It is never too early or too late to prioritize our financial well-being and establish a solid foundation for a comfortable retirement. Together, then, let us embark on this enlightening journey towards securing our financial independence and embracing the promise of a prosperous tomorrow.

WHAT IS A 401K?

A 401(k) is a type of retirement savings plan in the United States. It is named after a section of the U.S. Internal Revenue Code that governs this type of account. The primary purpose of a 401(k) plan is to provide individuals with a tax-advantaged way to save and invest for their retirement. Key characteristics of the 401(k) include the following:

- **Employer-sponsored:** 401(k) plans are typically offered by employers as part of their employee benefits package. The employer establishes the plan and may also provide matching contributions to encourage employees to save.
- **Employee contributions:** Employees can contribute a portion of their pre-tax salary to their 401(k) account. These contributions are not subject to income taxes at the time of contribution, which means they can reduce the employee's taxable income for that year.
- **Tax-deferred growth:** Money contributed to a 401(k) account grows on a tax-deferred basis, meaning you do not pay taxes on the investment gains or dividends if the money remains in the account. Taxes are only paid when you withdraw the funds, usually during retirement.
- **Contribution limits:** The Internal Revenue Service (IRS) sets annual contribution limits for 401(k) plans. The limits are subject to change but are designed to encourage individuals to save for retirement. At the time of writing, the limit for 2021 and 2022 is $19,500 for individuals under the age of 50. Those who are 50 years or older can make additional catch-up contributions.
- **Investment options:** The funds in a 401(k) can be invested in various financial instruments, such as stocks, bonds, mutual funds, and other investment vehicles. The specific investment options available depend on the plan offered by the employer.
- **Vesting:** Some employers impose a vesting schedule, which means employees gradually gain ownership of the employer's contributions over a specified period. Once fully vested, the employee retains the full value of the employer's contributions.

- **Early withdrawal penalties:** Generally, you cannot withdraw money from your 401(k) before age 59½ without incurring penalties, except in certain qualifying circumstances. If you withdraw funds early, you may be subject to income taxes and a 10% early withdrawal penalty.

It's important to note that the rules and regulations surrounding 401(k) plans may vary slightly depending on the specific plan and the employer. Because of this, it is recommended that you consult with a financial advisor or human resources department to understand the details of your specific 401(k) plan.

PENSIONS

A pension is a financial arrangement in which an individual receives regular income payments even after retiring from work. It is designed to provide individuals with a steady and secure source of income during their retirement years, ensuring they can maintain a certain standard of living without worrying where the next paycheck is coming from. They help individuals maintain their lifestyle, cover living expenses, and enjoy a comfortable retirement after they stop working.

Pensions can be offered by employers as part of an employment package or can be obtained through a government-sponsored program. In an employer-sponsored plan, both the employee and the employer contribute funds towards the pension over the course of the individual's working years. These contributions are invested with the goal of increasing the funds over time. When a person reaches the age of retirement or meets specific criteria, they become qualified to receive pension payments. The amount of pension income they receive is typically based on factors like their salary, years of service, and the rules of the pension plan they belong to. These payments can be given in different ways, such as a monthly annuity, a single lump sum, or a combination of both options.

WHAT ARE SOME COMMON RETIREMENT

PLANS?

There are several retirements plans available that individuals can use to save and invest for their retirement. Here are some common retirement examples:

- **401k:** A 401(k) is an employer-sponsored retirement plan where employees can contribute a portion of their salary to a tax-advantaged investment account. Employers may also match a percentage of the employee's contributions. Contributions are typically made with pre-tax dollars, and the funds grow tax-deferred until withdrawal.

- **Individual Retirement Account (IRA):** An IRA is a personal retirement account that individuals can open and contribute to independently of their employer. There are two primary types of IRAs: traditional and Roth. With a traditional IRA, contributions may be tax-deductible, and the funds grow tax-deferred until withdrawal. With a Roth IRA, contributions are made with after-tax dollars, and qualified withdrawals in retirement are tax-free.

- **Roth 401(k):** Similar to a traditional 401(k), a Roth 401(k) is an employer-sponsored retirement plan. However, contributions are made with after-tax dollars, and qualified withdrawals in retirement are tax-free.

- **Simplified Employee Pension (SEP) IRA:** A SEP IRA is designed for self-employed individuals and small business owners. Contributions are made by the employer on behalf of the employee, and the contributions are tax-deductible. The funds grow tax-deferred until withdrawal.

- **Simple IRA:** A Simple IRA is another retirement plan option for small businesses. It allows both employers and employees to contribute to the plan. Employees can contribute a portion of their salary, and employers must either match the employee's contributions or make a fixed contribution. The contributions grow tax-deferred until withdrawal.

- **Pension plans:** Pension plans are retirement plans typically offered by employers. Employees receive a predetermined benefit based on factors such as years of service and salary history. Pension plans are less common these days but are still offered by some employers, particularly in the public sector.

- **Annuities:** Annuities are insurance contracts that provide regular income payments in retirement. They can be purchased from insurance companies and offer various options for income payout and investment growth. Annuities can be either immediate, where payments start immediately after the initial investment, or deferred, where payments begin at a future date.

It is crucial that you, the reader, understand that retirement plans vary considerably in terms of eligibility criteria, contribution limits, and tax considerations. To identify the most appropriate retirement plan for your personal situation, I would advise that you seek guidance from a financial advisor or tax professional. They can provide expert advice tailored to your specific circumstances.

IF YOUR JOB OFFER ANY RETIREMENTS PLANS, TAKE IT!

Retirement planning is an essential aspect of one's financial journey, and if your job offers any retirement plans, it is highly advisable to take advantage of them. Retirement plans are designed to help individuals build a nest egg and provide financial security during their golden years. There are countless reasons why it is an excellent idea to take advantage of any retirement plans that your employer is willing to offer. These include:

- **Tax advantages:** Many employer-sponsored retirement plans, such as 401(k)s or IRAs (Individual Retirement Accounts), offer tax benefits. Contributions to these plans are often tax-deductible, meaning you can reduce your taxable income by the amount you contribute. Additionally, the growth of investments within the retirement plan is tax-deferred, allowing your money to compound without immediate tax implications.
- **Employer contributions:** Various employers offer matching

contributions. This means that for every dollar you contribute, your employer will also contribute a certain percentage, up to a specified limit. Employer matching is essentially free money, and by not taking advantage of it, you may be leaving valuable benefits on the table.

- **Long-term savings and investment growth:** By participating in a retirement plan, you are actively setting aside a portion of your income for the future. Over time, through regular contributions and potential investment growth, your retirement savings can grow significantly.

- **Diversification and professional management:** Retirement plans often offer a range of investment options, allowing you to diversify your portfolio. This diversification helps mitigate risk by spreading your investments across various asset classes and industries. Additionally, retirement plans typically have professional fund managers who oversee the investment options, ensuring that your money is managed by experts in the field.

- **Financial security in retirement:** Taking advantage of retirement plans allows you to build a solid financial foundation for your retirement. By contributing to your retirement account, you are taking proactive steps towards ensuring a comfortable and secure future. Without this, you may be solely reliant on government benefits or face financial difficulties during your retirement years.

It is crucial to review the retirement plans offered by your employer and understand the terms and conditions, contribution limits, vesting schedules, and investment options available. Consult with a financial advisor if needed to make informed decisions about your retirement savings strategy. Start planning early, contribute consistently, and make the most of the retirement plans provided by your employer to secure a brighter future for yourself.

DO NOT WITHDRAW YOUR 401K BEFORE RETIREMENT

Withdrawing your 401(k) before retirement should be avoided unless you are facing extreme financial hardships or have a well-thought-out plan. I make this recommendation for a handful of reasons:

- **Tax implications:** If you withdraw money from your 401(k) before the age of 59½, you may be subject to early withdrawal penalties and income taxes. Typically, early withdrawals incur a 10% penalty in addition to the regular income tax you owe on the withdrawn amount. This can significantly reduce the value of your savings and hinder your long-term financial goals.

- **Lost growth potential:** The longer you keep your money invested in a 401(k) or similar retirement account, the more time it has to grow. Withdrawing funds prematurely means you miss out on potential compounding returns over the years.

- **Impact on retirement savings:** Your 401(k) is specifically designed to provide financial security during retirement. By withdrawing funds early, you deplete the amount available for your retirement years. As a result, you may need to save more aggressively or rely on other sources of income to make up for the shortfall.

- **Difficulty in rebuilding savings:** Rebuilding your retirement savings after an early withdrawal can be challenging. Once you withdraw funds, it becomes harder to catch up and accumulate a sufficient nest egg. Depending on your financial situation and market conditions, substantial time and effort may be needed to replenish the funds you withdrew, potentially delaying your retirement plans.

- **Unforeseen circumstances:** Life is unpredictable, and unexpected expenses or emergencies can arise at any time. By prematurely tapping into your retirement savings, you limit your ability to cope with unforeseen financial challenges. It is generally wiser to build a separate emergency fund to address immediate needs and keep your retirement savings for their intended purpose.

In conclusion, it is generally advisable to avoid withdrawing funds from your 401(k) before reaching retirement age. Instead, explore other options like adjusting your budget, reducing expenses, increasing your savings rate, or seeking additional income sources to meet your current financial needs. A financial advisor can provide valuable guidance on managing your finances and exploring alternative solutions. Preserve your 401(k) for its intended purpose and explore alternative solutions to address your immediate financial needs. By doing so, you increase the likelihood of achieving your long-term financial goals and enjoying a secure retirement. And with that, our journey together came to an end. I hope that this book serves as a valuable resource throughout your life, and I encourage you once again to select your next reading material from my list of recommendations at the end of this book. Happy learning!

Glossary

INSURANCE KEY TERMS

Types Of Life Insurance Policies

For the most part, there are two types of life insurance plans - either term or permanent plans or some combination of the two. Life insurers offer various forms of term plans and traditional life policies as well as "interest sensitive" products which have become more prevalent since the 1980's. In New York State, the Department of Financial Services must approve any life insurance policy before a company can issue it to consumers and New York Insurance Law provides for standard provisions that must be included in every policy.

Term Insurance

Term insurance provides protection for a specified period. This period could be as short as one year or provide coverage for a specific number of years such as 5, 10, 20 years or to a specified age such as 80 or in some cases up to the oldest age in the life insurance mortality tables. Policies are sold with various premium guarantees. The longer the guarantee, the higher the initial premium. If you die during the term period, the company will pay the face amount of the policy to your beneficiary. If you live beyond the term period you had selected, no benefit is payable. As a rule, term policies offer a death benefit with no savings element or cash value.

Premiums are locked in for the specified period under the policy terms. The premiums you pay for term insurance are lower at an earlier age as compared with the premiums you pay for permanent insurance, but term rates rise as you grow older. Term plans may be "convertible" to a permanent plan of insurance. The coverage can be "level" providing the same benefit until the policy expires or you can have "decreasing" coverage during the term period with the premiums remaining the same. If you do not pay the premium for your term insurance policy, it will generally lapse without cash value, as compared to a permanent type of policy that has a cash value component. Currently term insurance rates are very competitive and among the lowest historically experienced.

It should be noted that it is a widely held belief that term insurance is the least expensive pure life insurance coverage available. One needs to review the policy terms carefully to decide which term life options are suitable to meet your circumstances.

Types of Term Insurance

- **Renewable Term**. Renewable term plans give you the right to renew for another period when a term ends, regardless of the state of your health. With each new

215

term the premium is increased. The right to renew the policy without evidence of insurability is an important advantage to you. Otherwise, the risk you take is that your health may deteriorate, and you may be unable to obtain a policy at the same rates or even at all, leaving you and your beneficiaries without coverage.

- **Convertible Term**. Convertible term policies often permit you to exchange the policy for a permanent plan. You must exercise this option during the conversion period. The length of the conversion period will vary depending on the type of term policy purchased. If you convert within the prescribed period, you are not required to give any information about your health. The premium rate you pay on conversion is usually based on your "current attained age", which is your age on the conversion date. This type of policy often provides the maximum protection with the smallest amount of cash outlay.

- **Level or Decreasing Term**. Under a level term policy, the face amount of the policy remains the same for the entire period. With decreasing term, the face amount reduces over the period. The premium stays the same each year. Often such policies are sold as mortgage protection with the amount of insurance decreasing as the balance of the mortgage decreases. If the insured dies the proceeds of the policy can be used to pay off the mortgage.

- **Adjustable Premium**. Traditionally, insurers have not had the right to change premiums after the policy is sold. Since such policies may continue for many years, insurers must use conservative mortality, interest and expense rate estimates in the premium calculation. Adjustable premium insurance, however, allows insurers to offer insurance at lower "current" premiums based upon less conservative assumptions with the right to change these premiums in the future. The premium, however, can never be more than the maximum guaranteed premiums stated in the policy.

Permanent Insurance (Whole Life or Ordinary Life)

While term insurance is designed to provide protection for a specified time period, permanent insurance is designed to provide coverage for your entire lifetime. To keep the premium rate level, the premium at the younger ages exceeds the actual cost of protection. This extra premium builds a reserve (cash value) which helps pay for the policy in later years as the cost of protection rises above the premium. Whole life policies stretch the cost of insurance over a longer period in order to level out the otherwise increasing cost of insurance. Under some policies, premiums are required to be paid for a set number of years. Under other policies, premiums are paid throughout the policyholder's lifetime. The insurance company invests the excess premium dollars.

This type of policy, which is sometimes called cash value life insurance, generates a savings element. Cash values are critical to a permanent life insurance policy. The size of the cash value build-up differs from company to company. Sometimes, there is no correlation between the size of the cash value and the premiums paid. It is the cash value of the policy that can be accessed while the policyholder is alive.

The Commissioners 1980 Standard Ordinary Mortality Table (CSO) is the current table used in calculating minimum nonforfeiture values and policy reserves for ordinary life insurance policies. This table provides the minimum cash values that must be guaranteed in your policy.

The policy's essential elements consist of the premium payable each year, the death benefits payable to the beneficiary and the cash surrender value the policyholder would receive if the policy were surrendered prior to death. You may make a loan against the cash value of the policy at a specified rate of interest or a variable rate of interest but such outstanding loans, if not repaid, will reduce the death benefit.

In 1984 a new federal tax law required that for permanent insurance to enjoy preferred tax treatment it must provide coverage up to at least age 95, limit the amount of premium that may be paid in relation to the face amount of coverage and establish a minimum ratio between cash value and face amount of insurance. Many permanent policies will contain provisions which specify these tax requirements.

There are two basic categories of permanent insurance, traditional and interest-sensitive, each with several variations. In addition, each category is generally available in either fixed-dollar or variable form.

Traditional Whole Life

Traditional whole life policies are based upon long-term estimates of expense, interest and mortality. The premiums, death benefits and cash values are stated in the policy.

There are six basic variations of traditional permanent insurance:

- **Non-Participating Whole Life**: A non-participating whole life policy will give you a level premium and face amount during your entire life. The advantages of such a policy are its fixed costs and generally low out-of-pocket premium payments. The disadvantage is that it pays no dividends.

- **Participating Whole Life:** A participating whole life policy pays dividends. The dividends represent the favorable experience of the company and result from excess investment earnings, favorable mortality and expense savings. Dividends can be paid in cash, used to reduce premiums, left to accumulate at interest or used to purchase paid-up additional insurance. Dividends are not guaranteed.

- **Indeterminate Premium Whole Life:** An indeterminate premium whole life policy is like a non-participating whole life plan of insurance except that it provides for adjustable premiums. The company will charge a "current" premium based on its current estimate of investment earnings, mortality, and expense costs. If these estimates change in later years, the company will adjust the premium accordingly but never above the maximum guaranteed premium stated in the policy.

- **Economatic Whole Life:** An economatic whole life policy provides for a basic amount of participating whole life insurance with an additional supplemental coverage provided using dividends. This additional insurance usually is a combination of decreasing term insurance and paid-up dividend additions. Eventually, the dividend additions should equal the original amount of supplemental coverage. However, because dividends may not be sufficient to purchase enough paid-up additions at a future date, it is possible that at some future time there could be a substantial decrease in the amount of supplemental insurance coverage.

- **Limited Payment Whole Life** If you want to pay premiums for a limited time the limited payment whole life policy gives you lifetime protection but requires only a limited number of premium payments. Because the premiums are paid over a shorter span of time, the premium payments will be higher than under the **whole life plan.**

- **Single Premium Whole Life** Single premium whole life is limited payment life where one large premium payment is made. The policy is fully paid up and no further premiums are required. Many such policies have substantial surrender charges if you want to cash in the policy during the first few years. Since a substantial payment is involved, it should be viewed as an investment-oriented product.
  - Interest in single premium life insurance is primarily due to the tax-deferred treatment of the build-up of its cash values. Taxes will be incurred on the gain, however, when you surrender the policy. You may borrow on the cash value of the policy, but remember that you may incur a substantial tax bill when you surrender, even if you have

borrowed out all the cash value.

Interest Sensitive Whole Life

While insurers guarantee stated benefits on traditional contracts far into the future based on long-term and overall company experience, they allocate investment earnings differently on interest sensitive whole life in order to better reflect current fluctuations in interest rates. The advantage is that improvements in interest rates will be reflected more quickly in interest sensitive insurance than in traditional; the disadvantage, of course, is that decreases in interest rates will also be felt more quickly in interest sensitive whole life.

There are four basic interest sensitive whole life policies:

Universal Life The universal life policy is actually more than interest sensitive as it is designed to reflect the insurer's current mortality and expense as well as interest earnings rather than historic rates. Universal life works by treating separately the three basic elements of the policy: premium, death benefit and cash value. The company credits your premiums to the cash value account. Periodically the company deducts from the cash value account its expenses and the cost of insurance protection, usually described as the mortality deduction charge. The balance of the cash value account accumulates at the interest credited. The company guarantees a minimum interest rate and a maximum mortality charge. Some universal life policies also specify a maximum basis for the expense charge. These guarantees are usually very conservative. Current assumptions are critical to interest sensitive products such as Universal Life. When interest rates are high, benefit projections (such as cash value) are also high. When interest rates are low, these projections are not as attractive.

Universal life is also the most flexible of all the various kinds of policies. Because it treats the elements of the policy separately, universal life allows you to change or skip premium payments or change the death benefit more easily than with any other policy.

The policy usually gives you an option to select one or two types of death benefits. Under one option your beneficiaries received only the face amount of the policy, under the other they receive both the face amount and the cash value account. If you want the maximum amount of death benefit now, the second option should be selected.

You generally pay a planned premium designed to keep the policy in force for life, and accumulate cash value, based upon the interest and expense and mortality charges you assume. It is important that these assumptions be realistic because if they are not, you may have to pay more to keep the policy from decreasing or lapsing. On the other hand, if your experience is better then the assumptions, than you may be able in the future to skip a premium, to pay less, or to have the plan paid up at an early date.

You do not have to pay the planned premium, but if you pay less, the benefit may be more like term insurance, which is only in force for a limited time and builds no cash value. On the other hand, if you pay more, and your assumptions are realistic, it is possible to pay up the policy at an early date.

If you surrender a universal life policy you may receive less than the cash value account because of surrender charges which can be of two types. A front-end type policy will deduct a percentage of the premium paid, while a back-end type policy will deduct a more substantial charge but only if the policy is surrendered before a specified period, generally 10 years but which could be as long as 20 years. A back-end type policy would be preferable if you intend to maintain coverage, and the charge decreases with each year you continue the policy. Remember that the interest rate and expense and mortality charges payables initially are not guaranteed for the life of the policy.

Although this type of policy gives you maximum flexibility, you will need to actively manage the policy to maintain sufficient funding, especially because the insurance company can increase mortality and expense charges. You should remember that the mortality charges increase, as you become older.

Excess Interest Whole Life If you are not interested in all of the flexible features of Universal Life, some insurers offer fixed premium versions called excess interest whole life. The key feature is that premium payments are required when due just like traditional whole life. If premiums are paid when due, the policy will not lapse.

With the premium level fixed, any additional or excess interest credited, or better life insurance experience, will improve the cash value of the policy. The premium level will probably be comparable to traditional whole life policies. Cash value may be applied to pay future premium payments. This type of product maximizes the deferred tax growth of your cash value.

Current Assumption Whole Life Current assumption whole life is similar to a universal life policy but your company determines the amount of premium to be paid. The company sets the initial premium based upon its current estimate of future investment earnings and mortality experience and retains the contractual right to reevaluate its original estimates to increase or decrease your premium payments later. If premiums are increased, some policies let you decrease the face amount of coverage so that you can continue to pay the original premium. Current mortality and experience and investment earnings can be credited to the insurance policy either through the cash value account and/or the premium or dividend structure (depending on whether it is a stock or mutual company). Regardless, this type of policy has the following characteristics:

- The premiums are subject to change based on the experience (mortality, expenses, investment) of the company. The policyowner does not exercise control over the changes.
- The policyowner can use the cash value to make loans just as he/she would with any traditional ordinary life insurance policy.
- A minimum amount of cash value is guaranteed, just as with traditional ordinary life insurance.
- The death benefit does not fluctuate.

Single Premium Whole Life There are a few single premium life products, which determine the premium using the current interest rate assumption. You may be asked to make additional premium payments where coverage could terminate because the interest rate dropped. Your starting interest rate is fixed only for a year or in some cases three to five years. The guaranteed rate provided for in the policy is much lower (e.g., 4%). Another feature that is sometimes emphasized is the "no cost" loan. Companies will set the loan interest rate to be charged on policy loans equal to the rate that is being credited to the policy.

Variable Life

Most types of both traditional and interest sensitive life policies can be purchased on either a fixed-dollar or variable basis. On a fixed-dollar basis, premium, face amount and cash values are specified in dollar amounts.

On the variable basis, face amount and cash value are specified in units, and the value of the units may increase or decrease depending upon the investment results. You can allocate your premiums among various investment pools (like stock, bond, money market, mutual funds and real estate pools) depending on the amount of risk you are willing to assume in the hope of a higher return.

Traditional variable life provides a minimum guaranteed death benefit, but many universal variable life products do not, and should investment experience be bad, coverage will terminate if substantially higher premium payments are not made. Variable life is also made available on a single premium basis but if investment experience is poor additional premiums will be required.

Credit Life Insurance

Although you can obtain credit life insurance (term) as an individual, it is usually sold on a group basis to a creditor, such as a bank, finance company or a company selling high priced items on the installment plan. The policy generally pays the outstanding balance of the debt at the time of the borrower's death, subject to policy maximums. Debts covered in this way include: personal loans; loans to cover the purchase of appliances, motor vehicles, mobile homes, farm equipment; educational loans; bank credit and revolving check loans; mortgages loans; etc.

When you borrow from an organization that has a group credit life policy, the organization may require you to purchase credit life insurance or it may simply offer the protection as an additional service. In either case you must receive a certificate of insurance describing the provisions of the group policy and any insurance charge. Generally the maximum amount of coverage is $220,000 for a mortgage loan and $55,000 for all other debts. Credit life insurance need not be purchased from the organization granting the loan.

If you are covered under a group credit life policy and you terminate coverage by prepaying or defaulting on the loan, or if the group policy itself is terminated, you may be entitled to a partial refund of the premium you paid so check your certificate. If life insurance is required by a creditor as a condition for making a loan, you may be able to assign an existing life insurance policy, if you have one. However, you may wish to buy group credit life insurance in spite of its higher cost because of its convenience and its availability, generally without detailed evidence of insurability.

Monthly Debit Ordinary Insurance

This is insurance with premiums payable monthly which are meant to be collected by the agent at your home. In most cases, however, home collections are not made and premiums are mailed by you to the agent or to the company.

There are certain factors that tend to increase the costs of debit insurance more than regular life insurance plans:

- Certain expenses are the same no matter what the size of the policy, so that smaller policies issued as debit insurance will have higher premiums per $1,000 of insurance than larger size regular insurance policies.
- In some companies, more debit policyholders allow their policies to lapse than is generally the case with policyholders of regular life insurance. Since early lapses are expensive to a company, the costs must be passed on to all debit policyholders.
- Since debit insurance is designed to include home collections, higher commissions and fees are paid on debit insurance than on regular insurance. In many cases these higher expenses are passed on to the policyholder.
- As a general rule the combination of smaller amounts, higher lapse rates and higher commissions and fees on debit insurance tends to make it more expensive than comparable regular life insurance plans.

Where a company has different premiums for debit and regular insurance it may be possible for you to purchase a larger amount of regular insurance than debit at no extra cost. Therefore, if you are thinking of debit insurance, you should certainly investigate regular life insurance as a cost-saving alternative.

Modified Life Plan

A modified life plan is similar to whole life except that you pay a lower premium for the first few years and a higher than regular whole life premium in later years. This plan is designed for those who cannot initially afford the regular whole life premium but who want the higher premium coverage and feel they will eventually be able to pay the higher premium.

The Family Policy

The family policy is a combination plan that provides insurance protection under one contract to all members of your immediate family husband, wife and children. Usually family policies are sold in units (packages) of protection, such as $5,000 on the main wage earner, $1,500 on the spouse and $1,000 on each child.

Joint Life and Survivor Insurance

Joint Life and Survivor Insurance provides coverage for two or more persons with the death benefit payable at the death of the last of the insureds. Premiums are significantly lower under joint life and survivor insurance than for policies that insure only one person, since the probability of having to pay a death claim is lower.

Joint Life Insurance

Joint Life Insurance provides coverage for two or more persons with the death benefit payable at the first death. Premiums are significantly higher than for policies that insure one person, since the probability of having to pay a death claim is higher.

Endowment Insurance

Endowment insurance provides for the payment of the face amount to your beneficiary if death occurs within a specific period of time such as twenty years, or, if at the end of the specific period you are still alive, for the payment of the face amount to you. Due to recent tax law changes many endowment plans no longer qualify as life insurance for tax purposes and are generally not being offered by insurers.

Juvenile insurance

Juvenile insurance provides a minimum of protection and could provide coverage, which might not be available at a later date. Amounts provided under such coverage are generally limited based on the age of the child. The current limitations for minors under the age of 14.5 would be the greater of $50,000 or 50% of the amount of life insurance in force upon the life of the applicant. The limitations on a minor under the age of 4.5 would be the greater of $50,000 or 25% of the amount of life insurance in force upon the life of the applicant. Juvenile insurance may be sold with a payor benefit rider, which provides for waiving future premiums on the child's policy in the event of the death of the person who pays the premium.

Senior Life Plans

Senior life insurance, sometimes referred to as graded death benefit plans, provides eligible older applicants with minimal whole life coverage without a medical examination. Since such policies are issued with little or no underwriting they will provide only for a return of premium or minimum graded benefits if death occurs during a specified period which is generally the first two or three policy years. The permissible issue ages for this type of coverage range from ages 50 75. The maximum issue amount of coverage is $25,000. These policies are usually more expensive than a fully underwritten policy if the person qualifies as a standard risk.

Pre-need Insurance

This type of coverage is for a small face amount, typically purchased to pay the burial expenses of the insured. As previously mentioned within the discussion of monthly debit ordinary insurance, this coverage often carries a higher premium per $1,000 of coverage than larger size policies.

RETIREMENT GLOSSARY

Retirement fund

A retirement fund[1], generally speaking, is a special account either sponsored by your employer or established on your own to invest contributions for future retirement income.

401(k)

A 401(k) is an employer-sponsored retirement savings plan. It's also known as a defined contribution plan. This plan allows employees to make regular contributions that are tax-deductible to an investment account for use in retirement. Contributions have a maximum annual contribution limit set by the Internal Revenue Service (IRS).

Matching contributions

Many employers also offer a 401(k)-matching program, where the employer will set a predetermined amount to match employee contributions. For example, the employer might match $.50 for every contributed dollar up to a specified percentage of your income.

Individual retirement account (IRA)

An IRA is an investment account for retirement saving. These accounts have a set annual contribution limit defined by the IRS.
IRAs are "tax-advantaged," meaning they have tax benefits, which depend on the type of IRA you choose. Once you hit the age of 59 1/2, you can begin withdrawing from your IRA. If you withdraw before that age, you will face additional tax penalties.

---

1. https://www.protective.com/learn/retirement-funds-101

Traditional IRA

One type of IRA is a Traditional IRA. It is a tax-deferred retirement option, meaning you make contributions with your pre-tax dollars and don't pay taxes until the money is disbursed. You are taxed at your current income tax rate at the time of withdrawal.

Traditional IRAs have set annual contribution limits, and you must begin to take your required minimum distributions (RMDs) by age 72.

Roth IRA

Another type of IRA is a Roth IRA[2]. With a Roth IRA, you contribute after-tax dollars. However, you can withdraw your contributions — the money you put into the account — anytime without taxes or penalties. Earnings on contributions can also be withdrawn without taxes or penalties, however, only if the conditions set forth by the IRS are met.

As with other types of investment accounts, the IRS determines the maximum yearly contributions you can make. Moreover, Roth IRAs don't have any RMD requirements.

Learn more about distributions from individual retirement accounts from the IRS.[3]

Pre-tax retirement accounts

A pre-tax retirement account[4] is an account for which you do not pay taxes on your contributions or earnings until you begin withdrawing from them. For many, the benefit of this type of account is that contributions made up to the IRS-declared annual contribution limit are exempt from federal income tax for that year.

After-tax retirement accounts

With an after-tax retirement account, the contributions you withdraw are not taxed. This is because you have already paid taxes on your contributions, as they have been made with after-tax dollars.

2. https://www.protective.com/learn/what-is-the-difference-between-roth-and-traditional-ira

3. https://www.irs.gov/publications/p590b#en_US_2019_pub-link1000231059https_853ae90f0351324bd73ea615e6487517__6666cd76f96956469e7be39d750cc7d9__6666cd76f9695 6469e7be39d750cc7d9_www.irs.gov_6666cd76f96956469e7be39d750cc7d9_publica- tions_6666cd76f96956469e7be39d750cc7d9_p590b_01abfc750a0c942167651c40d088531d_en_US_2019_pub- link1000231059https_853ae90f0351324bd73ea615e6487517__6666cd76f96956469e7be39d750cc7d9__6666cd76f9695 6469e7be39d750cc7d9_www.irs.gov_6666cd76f96956469e7be39d750cc7d9_publica- tions_6666cd76f96956469e7be39d750cc7d9_p590b_01abfc750a0c942167651c40d088531d_en_US_2019_pub- link1000231059_9371d7a2e3ae86a00aab4771e39d255d_

4. https://www.protective.com/learn/understanding-the-difference-between-pre-tax-and-after-tax

Pension plan

A pension plan[5] is another type of retirement plan. It's also called a defined benefit plan. With this type of retirement plan, your employer funds and invests contributions for you. They also define the income that you will get from the pool of investments based on a set calculation that can include total earnings, age and years worked at the company.

Retirement annuity

With a retirement annuity[6], you pay a lump sum or a series of payments to an insurance company, and, in return, the company will pay you a lump sum or series of payments for a predetermined number of years or for the rest of your life.

Many use retirement annuities to provide a stable source of income during retirement.

Annuities are intended as vehicles for long-term retirement planning, which is why withdrawals reduce an annuity's remaining death benefit, contract value, cash surrender value and future earnings. Annuities also may be subject to income tax and, if taken prior to age 59 ½, an additional 10% IRS tax penalty may apply.

BOOK RECOMMENDATIONS

1. *Balance* by Toure Roberts
2. *6 Months to 6 Figures* by Peter J Vogid
3. *He-Motions* by TD Jakes
4. *The Courage to Live Your Dreams* by Les Brown
5. *The Power of Positive Thinking* by Norman Vincent Peale
6. *The Audacity of Hope* by Barack Obama
7. *The Ultimate Zig Ziglar Library* by Zig Ziglar
8. *Think Big* by Ben Carson
9. *Gifted Hands* by Ben Carson
10. *The Purpose of a Driven Life* by Rick Warren
11. *No Disrespect* by Sister Souljah

---

5. https://www.protective.com/learn/what-is-the-difference-between-a-pension-and-a-retirement-plan

6. https://www.protective.com/learn/what-is-an-annuity

Don't miss out!

Visit the website below and you can sign up to receive emails whenever www.thefinancialguidelines.com publishes a new book. There's no charge and no obligation.

https://books2read.com/r/B-A-HNCZ-SXXKC

BOOKS 2 READ

Connecting independent readers to independent writers.

Printed in the USA
CPSIA information can be obtained
at www.ICGtesting.com
JSHW021051200923
48470JS00008B/34